SO-CCA-575

"Incredible as it seems, extraterrestrial beings visited this planet over 4000 years ago. The result of their visit almost caused the total annihilation of the human race as we know it. Only eight persons survived.

"Now as we ponder our own destiny, signs in the heavens point to a new invasion. Will they come in peace? Will the human race survive or become extinct? If indeed we are captured or for some unknown reason are able to make peace with these creatures, what will be the results when the Sons of God return?

"This book presents answers to the most formidable crisis ever to challenge the sons of man."
—Kelly L. Segraves

H. W. Wall.
Nov. 25.

SONS OF GOD RETURN

Kelly L. Segraves

SPIRE BOOKS

Fleming H. Revell Company • Old Tappan, New Jersey

All Bible quotations are from The King James Bible
unless otherwise noted.

SONS OF GOD RETURN

A SPIRE BOOK
Published by Pyramid Publications for the
Fleming H. Revell Company

Spire Books edition published June, 1975

Copyright © 1975 by Kelly L. Segraves
All Rights Reserved

Library of Congress Catalog Card Number: 75–4464

Printed in the United States of America

SPIRE BOOKS are published by
Fleming H. Revell Company
Old Tappan, New Jersey 07675, U.S.A.

CONTENTS

INTRODUCTION   9

CHAPTER ONE   The Concept   13

CHAPTER TWO   The Contactee   25

CHAPTER THREE   The Claims   45

CHAPTER FOUR   The Message   59

CHAPTER FIVE   The Meaning   87

CHAPTER SIX   The Key   111

CHAPTER SEVEN   The Problem   127

CHAPTER EIGHT   The Deception   151

CHAPTER NINE   The Result   167

BIBLIOGRAPHY   187

SONS OF GOD RETURN

INTRODUCTION

The sighting of flying saucers is commonplace in our society. Over five million people have reported seeing some type of UFOs. It is claimed that a saucer is sighted every 15-20 minutes. Numerous reports of UFO activity by qualified individuals certainly lends credence to the concept that flying saucers are real. Many claims have been made by concerned citizens as to the purpose of these extraterrestrial visitations. Scientists themselves are finally waking up to the UFO problem as new attempts to understand this baffling phenomena unfold.

A group of San Diego scientists and engineers are engaged in the production of a new supersensitive magnotometer to detect electromagnetic fields. The magnotometer is coupled with four other sensing devices. This group known as Precision Monitoring Systems hopes to gain physical and objective evidence to support visual sightings in order to accurately determine what UFO's are all about.

The civilian-run Aerial Phenomena Research Organization (APRO) and the Mutual Unidentified Flying Object Network (MUFON) have bases in Southern California. On a national basis more than 500 ranking scientists support these two organizations. Many noted men—such as the vice-president of a Los Angeles aerospace giant and a multi-degreed bio-physicist at a San Diego University—lend support, but ask that their names remain anonymous.

One thing is clear. As Dr. James Harder, engineer and specialist in fluid mechanics of the University of California says, "I know of no scientist who's become professionally involved with UFO investigation who doesn't believe in extraterrestrial phenomena."

This then is the crux of the UFO issue—extraterrestrial life. Does it exist and if so, where? Are these aliens friendly? If so, what is their mission and interest in the planet Earth? These are the pertinent questions in a proper understanding of the great flying saucer phenomenon now gracing the skies of our world. It is the express purpose of this book to examine the evidence of modern saucer visitations as well as ancient records in order to determine the identity of these extraterrestrial visitors. It will then be our task to predict as accurately as possible the results of these visitations and the future of this planet when the Sons of God Return.

ONE

The Concept

"As I entered my driveway I noticed a light following me in the rearview mirror. After parking the car in the garage I noticed that the light source was slightly above the garage door and shone a strange luminous blue. Stepping outside I was shocked by the eerie character of the tiny egg-shaped object which emitted this strange light. It was a little larger than a football and fuzzy around the edges because of the foggy light. It hovered, darted, and swooped, all the while giving the distinct impression it was studying me. After a few minutes it shot out of the driveway and streaked off into the wooded night."

This is certainly a fascinating description of a strange and foreign object observing mankind. This is typical of many sightings of small luminous objects that grace our skies. Could these be manned observations by intelligent beings smaller than a man's hand? Some people believe they are creatures with a supertechnology who have traveled from somewhere beyond the Milky Way to observe God's experiment with man on the planet Earth. Others feel that these small objects are remote controlled observation discs used by intelligent beings to record the actions of people from a safe distance. In light of the numerous sightings by literally millions of people who claim to have seen unidentified flying objects it becomes imperative for us to examine the evidence in order to understand fully the impact of this visitation of saucer people.

Flying saucers come in all sizes and shapes, which may be one of the reasons the average man has failed to grasp the impact of these sightings. Rather than attempt to document the numerous sightings we will instead accept them at face value and therefore survey the various types of craft in an attempt to gain insight into these visitations. Experts tell us that all UFOs do not have a common origin and therefore we should not expect them all to be alike.

Most UFO sightings at night describe the objects as luminous, glowing lights easily mistaken for a star with the exception that they sometimes change colors. In-flight saucers often exhibit erratic flight patterns—swooping, darting, zigzagging, swaying. It is said that occasionally saucers appear to hover in the night skies duplicating exactly the appearance of stars. They may even maintain their relative position for days against the background of stars.

The most frequently sighted saucer is the disc-like object ranging in size from a few feet to as much as four hundred feet in diameter. Although size would be hard to determine and is sometimes dependent on the ability of the observer to estimate the range, speed, distance, and size in a matter of seconds, the common size of these disc-like objects is believed to be between fifteen and forty-five feet in diameter.

One type of disc-shaped UFO looks like a straw hat. Photographs of such an object were taken in 1965 by a highway traffic investigator for the Orange County Road Department. The estimated size of the saucer was approximately thirty feet in diameter and eight feet in thickness. It gave the appearance of polished metal with a narrow belt of light sweeping around the lower surfaces. The belt seemed to reach the outer edge of the craft, according to Rex Heflin, the man who took the photos. The object skimmed over telephone poles, crossed the road in front of him, and continued flying at a low level. Heflin estimated that the sighting had taken fifteen seconds during which time four Polaroid photographs were taken of the disc-shaped object. The original photos were sent to *Life* magazine to be examined but were returned with the notation that they were too controversial to be published. Later the photographs were published by the *Santa Ana Register* and released to other papers by United Press International. Heflin's report is contained in the official U.S. Air

Force Project Blue Book report. Although there seems little evidence that the photographs were faked, the official Air Force conclusion is that they are a hoax. Their conclusion was based on the fact that one could throw an object into the air, photograph it, and call it a flying saucer since the photographs show only something flying through the air.

It seems obvious to those who have examined the Air Force report in order to establish the reliability of the sighting that little if any attention was given by the Air Force to determine the true nature of the object. They seem more intent on explaining away this particular sighting. It is generally agreed among advocates of UFOlogy that the government agencies are not releasing all the facts. Such an attitude has created an unofficial force of investigators, some of whom are members of military and government agencies, who are disenchanted with the cover-up tactics of the military. These people are engaging in private investigations of government files in order to reevaluate the official positions taken in the past. Such investigations lend strong support to the reality of Heflin's saucer, at least enough to cause us to continually examine the evidence in order to predict the results of such visitations or implications. The straw hat type of saucer is but one of several large disc-shaped UFOs.

Another type is the flattened saucer encircled by a large ring. This configuration is reminiscent of the planet Saturn for which it is named. This type of craft has been photographed on several different occasions. People who have seen this type of object describe its flight as similar to a bat's and say that it gives off a greenish haze. Other types of disc-like objects have been sighted and photographed. Some of these have a round dome, while others have a flattened dome on top with an antenna-like structure protruding upward next to the dome. Other sightings of disc-like UFOs describe the object as looking like two saucers joined at the rims with the lower section giving a flatter appearance than the upper. Some experts feel this type of craft may account for the brightly glowing globes that are frequently sighted in our evening skies. Because of the intense light given off by these craft the details of the structure are obscure and yet it is possible to discern an upper and lower section of the light.

Although there are many viewpoints as to the origin of various types of saucers, a large segment of interested proponents of UFOlogy feel that the disc-like objects are scout ships sent from cigar-shaped mother ships. This larger type of craft is regularly reported to be shaped like a giant cigar or cylinder. Again the size of these cigar-shaped UFOs varies and estimates may be subject to the ability of the individual to make quick guesses. On many occasions these pulsating reddish objects have been observed to receive and send out disc-like UFOs, thus supporting the concept that they are mother ships.

Ideas about the meanings of these sightings and visitations range from statements that each saucer type contains a visitor from a different galaxy to the concept that these are angels or demons (intelligent beings which are considered gods). Some people claim that these are beings from the future sent back in time to observe their own beginnings, while other people hold to the concept that we are observing some type of travel into a fourth dimension of which we have little, if any, understanding. It becomes apparent that the flying saucer phenomenon is very real. We add to this evidence the sighting of small egg-shaped UFOs, such as the object described in the beginning of this chapter. It certainly fills the imagination with fear and wonder as to the significance of the objects that grace our skies. There have been many books written to explain this phenomenon and many attempts to understand the technology that must be involved in this type of space travel.

The flight capacities of these UFOs are awesome. Saucers that appear as glowing lights are said to have observed each of our space shots. Russian astronauts reportedly saw a type of UFO during their oribts of the earth. Similar reports have been given by many of the American astronauts during the Apollo missions. Although it would be hard to determine, actual observers claim that the speed at which these objects travel borders on the miraculous. It is not uncommon to hear of speeds of two to three thousand miles per hour. Yet these same objects are sometimes observed to be almost stationary. This wide range of capabilities certainly lends credence to the concept that these crafts are extraterrestrial in origin. One pilot observed a UFO apparently monitoring his aircraft. This particular UFO suddenly disappeared from view with incredible speed only to return a few seconds later with a sister ship. Comments like these from reliable sources raise the question of communication between the craft. Was it necessary to go and fetch the sister ship or is it simply easier than standard communication? When tracking UFOs, Air Force pilots have reported their amazing ability to make seemingly impossible ninety degree turns, thereby making them extremely difficult to track. What seems confusing is the lack of radar support for sightings of these objects by reliable witnesses such as Air Force pilots. As hard as it is to explain the incredible number of sightings, the apparent lack of empirical evidence presents us with one of the most baffling mysteries of all time.

Michael Thomas, a Santa Ana, California, steelworker, encountered a huge object while driving to visit his brother. It was a clear morning when Thomas sighted an object as big as a diesel truck coming down the road. It was glowing orange with gray on top and traveled about fifteen feet above the ground. He indicated that his radio turned to static. The object came so close he thought he would hit it. Naturally he slammed on his brakes, causing the car to turn around and stall. Terrified, he jumped out and hid under the car. Looking out from underneath the car he noted the object was still glowing and humming loudly. Thomas described the UFO as resembling a partially deflated football, a flat disc shape. Running down the road for help he met Bill Alderson, a ranger of the California Forestry Division. He had been driving behind Thomas. Alderson reported that Thomas was trembling and incoherent, obviously terrified. When they reached Thomas' car the motor had boiled over but the object was gone. Thomas reported that the UFO left at high speed in an eastward direction and vanished over the hills when he fled. Since the car's motor had been overhauled recently and Thomas was driving on flat ground there is no apparent reason for the engine to have boiled over. The fact that the car's metal turned hot is still a mystery.

In California, near the area of Big Bear Lake, large numbers of sightings of flying saucers occurred in late 1973. So many people have had a close look at three very big UFOs that warnings have been published not to shoot at them. Over forty sightings have been made by reliable sober people who live around the lake. It has been reported that many of these objects are flying at treetop level. One housewife suffered acute pressure in the eardrums when one giant ship flashed past one hundred yards from her home. Mrs. Acosta reported that her daughter suffered an immediate nose bleed. A newspaper freelance writer, Joey Sherman, saw a UFO at close range when it passed by his home. He stated that they watched it with binoculars. It was golden in color and ball shaped. "It was the wildest thing you can imagine," he said. His body turned cold. Scientists at

Big Bear Solar Observatory state that they intend to observe the objects under a magnified condition if the UFOs continue to appear in the vicinity.

Saucer activity is becoming commonplace in the United States. Gary J. Chopic, Los Angeles consultant for a major oil company, was driving home in October 1973 when he saw a grayish-pink vehicle settle into a vale near the road. The object was only one hundred feet away and Chopic said he had a five-minute view of the object. It was approximately fifty feet long and thirty feet wide and hovered approximately ten feet off the ground. There were no visible windows or doors but it carried an insignia which he described as a huge "V" with smaller "v"s inside the larger one. Topping off the craft was a bubble of glass-like substance about eight feet long and one foot in diameter. Chopic then saw one of the first humanoids or space men reported in California by a witness deemed reliable by phenomena investigators. He said an individual came from the opposite side of the machine, looked up toward him and scrambled to the other side of the craft and disappeared. The being appeared to be of normal human appearance wearing something similar to a wet suit, though the color was perhaps silver. The shocked Chopic could not determine any of the facial features of the being. After a clicking sound was heard the vehicle made a whirring or humming noise as a misty, light substance appeared and enveloped the craft. Chopic says he smelled something sweet, similar to incense, then the object was gone—just disappearing from his sight. Law officials from Simi Valley investigated Chopic's story and although they found no evidence of the UFO they considered him a sober and reliable witness. "I am not a believer in flying saucers," he said, "but I have no explanation whatever for what I saw." A scientist at the California Institute of Technology who asked that his name be withheld theorizes that another civilization has the ability to materialize and dematerialize at will, which would explain UFOs that do not fly off but simply vanish.

It was two thirty in the morning when Robert Klinn turned into his driveway in a beach community in California. He had been working late at the lab viewing a motion picture of a UFO taken by a scientist in Montana. As he parked his car a neighbor ran over and pointed out a large yellowish-white glowing blob moving slowly above the horizon over the beach. Entering the house they obtained a telescope and focused it on the object. For the next hour and twenty-seven minutes they watched the lights that made up this glowing object flash and change positions, sometimes forming bisecting lines, at other times forming triangles. Eventually the lights began entering a cigar-shaped object that had appeared on the scene. As the lights came together there was a tremendous flare up of light. After the larger object moved back and forth a while all movement stopped, the lights flickered and went off.

Mrs. Sarah Thompson of Franklin, Kentucky, tells of a terrifying experience. She was followed by a huge, glowing, hissing UFO. With trembling hands she gripped her steering wheel and became barely able to drive. Her small son whimpered on the seat beside her. She had never seen a flying saucer before and hopes never to see one again. She was driving across town to see some relatives when she saw an oblong, football-shaped object. It glowed red all over and made a low hissing sound. The incident, which took place in October 1973, nearly scared Mrs. Thompson and her son to death as the object followed the car. Upon reaching her destination Mrs. Thompson called the police. Police sergeant Robert Baird entered the area; he reported also seeing a round, orange-colored object which flew out of sight as he watched it. He did not hear any sound from the object itself. In this same area policeman Dave Powell followed a UFO that was about two thousand feet in the air and a half-mile away. He and sergeant Dan Pinson saw it from their patrol car. They radioed to headquarters and reported seeing the orange-shaped object. There were two helicopters in the area. One chopper began to follow the thing but before it got close the UFO sped off after circling the city twice. Again they reportedly heard no sound from the object. A photograph was taken which shows what appears to be a series of lights forming a triangle. At this time the UFO was just above the horizon but suddenly stopped and zigzagged back and forth the way a ball bounces, Powell stated. About three minutes later they headed east but lost contact with the object after a brief chase. One local man saw the UFO several times on different nights. He called the police the first time he spotted it. Johnny Drake, a welder, said the object was about fifteen feet in the air and had red, white, and blue flashing lights. It bounced all over the sky at great speeds and then flew out of sight. It is curious that Mrs. Thompson's home is in the same area where United States military planes mysteriously exploded and crashed while chasing a UFO some twenty years ago.

In Paso Robles, California, a Marine Corps Vietnam veteran and his friend, a computer analyst, sighted a hovering UFO on December 14, 1973. The object is reported to have had a conical protrusion that was showing a steady flame-like beam to the ground. This caused an elliptical area of ground to glow. After the object departed at an incredible speed, the contacted ground continued to glow. The two observers ran over to investigate. Two six-foot, glowing humanoids were spotted. These robot-like creatures were illuminated by a flashlight and seen standing between the men and the area of earth that had been bombarded by the beam of light from the UFO. These creatures were aluminum-colored, cylindrical shapes that were shaking their arms or appendages. They disappeared immediately and the ground suddenly stopped glowing.

In spite of the variety and quantity of sightings, basic questions still must be answered: Where do these saucers come from? How are they powered, and by whom? What is the purpose of these visitations? When contact with human beings is made what is the message? In order to determine to the best of our ability the answers to these questions, it becomes necessary first of all to examine the claims of the contactees.

TWO

The Contactee

"The road was dark and lonely as I hurried down the bleak highway toward my home in upper New York. Suddenly I noticed a brilliant red glow inside my car. Thinking I was speeding I looked in the rearview mirror for the police and saw nothing but this red light covering everything. As I rounded a bend in the road a bright, brilliant red object appeared to my left over a telephone pole. It must have been fifty to sixty feet in diameter with a dome-like thing on top with red and green lights underneath. I was terrified."

Such is the report of a woman's frantic plight on a deserted highway near Ithaca, New York, in the early 1960s. The object extended a wide beam of light which completely took control of her car, causing it to stop. She became hysterical but could not scream. She reported that her eyes were hurting and burning and she had difficulty in swallowing, probably from being so frightened. She was worried because of her child in the back seat—she thought of running but there was no place to go, no other cars around. The only house seemed to be more than a mile away across an open field. She continually attempted to put the car in motion, stepping on the accelerator, but it did not work. The red and green lights on the disc-shaped object continued to flash in all directions. The car began to move, not forward but sideways. The object was controlling her vehicle, forcing it off the side of the road. No matter how she tried, she could not stop the graddual movement of the car past the shoulder of the road some five feet into a field of alfalfa. The lights inside her car had become dim. The headlights, which had been clearly visible with the high beams on, dimmed to nothingness. Only the red and green flashes from the object accented the dark sky. The car was still in drive but the motor had stopped. Nothing could propel the car forward. She was helpless.

A strange noise began to emanate from the object. It

sounded almost exactly like a television antenna vibrating in the wind, giving off a low humming sound similar to the sound of a swarm of bees. Suddenly the sound stopped and she began to hear voices. This was a strange phenomena, considering that the wind was blowing, the car windows were rolled up, and there were flurries of snow in the air. In the midst of the howling wind a chorus of voices gave a clear message of impending danger. It was spoken in broken English, as if the words were being translated. Slowly came a warning of death to a local resident who would be killed in a specific city in a tractor-trailer owned by a friend. These were not impressions in her mind, but real voices. Although the man who was to die was not known by the contactee she did know his sister.

She was told her son would not remember anything from the time the car stopped until it left the highway. After several minutes the terrifying experience came to a close. Gradually her car moved itself back out to the road. She reported that the steering wheel actually turned as if someone were sitting there instead of her. It came to the proper position on the road in the right-hand lane. The motor started, her lights became operative, and the car began to function under the control of the object in the sky.

After several minutes of controlled driving they entered another stretch of road. The white beam of light from underneath the object vanished as they began to move down the highway, leaving only the blinking red and green lights on the bottom rim of the object. They were so bright it was hard to tell whether they were round or square. The red lights were more prominent, but the colors were intermingled. Her vehicle remained under the control of the object in the air until she noticed other cars coming toward her. Then the object vanished.

She found herself alone and in control of her vehicle,

driving against traffic and trying to relax. Her child in the back seat remembered nothing of the experience.

After returning home she had difficulty sleeping and awoke screaming upon hearing a low humming sound. The cause of the sound was discovered to be a television antenna vibrating because of the strong wind. In her sleep it sounded like the humming sound from the object before the voices began talking.

The next day she heard the news from her sister that the man whose name had been given her by the chorus of voices had been killed in the exact city mentioned and in a tractor-trailer owned by the friend specified. This was certainly a frightening experience to the woman, and it is one which may give us some insight into the prophetic nature of the saucer contacts.

Contact with saucerians has taken place on numerous occasions in a variety of different settings. In some instances the individual will see a saucer and hear voices while in other cases visual contact is made with the extraterrestrial visitors. One incident occurred in Ontario, Canada, in the middle of 1950. A husband and wife on vacation were interrupted by what they termed a strange vibration of the air. They felt as if there had been an explosion except that there had been no sound. Climbing up a rock formation close to the beach where they were picnicking, the husband sighted a curious disc-shaped object some four hundred yards in the distance. It was floating in the water as if it were made of a light metal like aluminum. He described it as looking like two saucers joined at the rim with portholes on the rim itself. The object was reported to shine brightly in the noonday sun. After his wife had joined him the couple estimated the diameter of the object to be about fifty feet.

As they watched they were taken aback by seeing little creatures walking about on top of the craft engaged in some type of work. At the center of the craft there appeared to be a rotating antenna which was operated by one of these saucerians. Their movement was described as robot-like; they turned their heads before turning their feet and stopped when the antenna stopped. The witnesses stated that the antenna always stopped when it pointed to the rock formation where they were hiding. When they dropped out of sight behind the rock the antenna continued its rotation and the saucerians resumed their work. Strange as this claim may be it is substantiated by other sightings of small creatures and floating disc-shaped objects in various parts of the world. Experts believe that the antenna-like object picks up brain waves; this explains the reaction of the saucerians when individuals watching them are spotted.

In other sightings where contact is made the saucerians seem to possess the ability to read the mind of the individual. An evidence of this fact is the classic case of Barney and Betty Hill. The Hills were driving in their car when they noticed a bright object ahead of them. The sky appeared to be clear and this luminous object was strange because of its shape and the density of its lights compared to the stars behind it. After a few minutes they stopped their car and continued to watch through binoculars the fast-moving object. It then stopped and hovered in the air. As they watched the hovering object, wing-like objects appeared from the body of the object with red lights on their tips. The object came toward them until it was within a few feet of their car. At this point they decided to flee from the area as fast as possible. Mr. Hill was driving and Mrs. Hill continued to watch through an open window. They said that while the object was hovering above them they heard a series of short loud buzzes which they described as sounding like someone dropping a tuning fork. They reported they could not feel any vibrations from these buzzing sounds. Visual contact with the object was lost and they continued on their journey. Later they heard the buzzing sound of the object again, but did not see it.

The flying pattern of the saucer was very erratic as the object changed directions rapidly, ascending and descending numerous times in a very jerky manner. As a civil service employee in a Boston post office Mr. Hill admits that he possesses no scientific or technical training. He and his wife had not intended to report this incident but because they both saw the same things they decided it might be important. He feels the whole incident was incredible and still finds it hard to believe that such a thing could happen. The fact that both he and his wife had the same experience gives them some sense of its reality.

The Air Force officials at Peace Air Force Base who investigated the case concluded their report by stating that the information was obtained by a telephone conversation, therefore the reliability of the observers could not be judged. "He seemed apparently honest and serious about the sighting," they said.

Shockingly, the Hills discovered later that there was a time lapse of some two hours that was unaccounted for between the two periods of buzzing sounds. As a result of this experience the Hills experienced a series of strange nightmares, which led them to seek psychiatric help. The psychiatrist discovered the root of the problem and traced the origin of the nightmares to the missing two hours. Under hypnosis, the Hills claimed to have been taken aboard a flying saucer.

Consciously the individuals did not remember anything more than the sighting of the saucer, but the events of their abduction and examination by a saucer crew seem very believable when recalled under hypnosis. Reportedly Barney Hill sighted the saucer a few hundred feet away and remembers watching it through binoculars. He saw a humanoid whom he thought was

their leader and remembers communicating with it
through a type of telepathy. In this exchange of ideas
and thoughts, Hill was reminded of hunting rabbits
while a boy and recalled how he and his sister had cor-
nered and captured a rabbit who thought he was safe.
Hill related this incident to himself and was given the
assurance by the saucer people that he was not a rabbit
and would be kept safe. Later Barney and Betty Hill
were taken aboard the saucer and completely examined. It is believed by some that the purpose of this examination by the saucerians was to make duplicates of
these individuals and that possibly in some remote
galaxy in our universe duplicates of Barney and Betty
Hill are roaming free populating new worlds. Of
course, such a conclusion is mere speculation but it is
interesting to note that an extensive examination of individuals by saucerians is not uncommon. Reportedly
these saucer people have examined examples of cows,
rabbits, horses, dogs, and other animals, as well as
plants, for purposes unknown. Individuals claim that
they have been given rides in saucers visiting other
parts of our solar system. In the case of Barney and
Betty Hill special attention was given to the female
anatomy in what many conclude is an attempt to understand the reproductive system.

The Hills were contacted by a group of creatures
who came upon them after their car was stopped. One
of the creatures opened the door for Mrs. Hill and
pointed something at her. Betty Hill described him as
being approximately her height, around five to five and
one-half feet tall. They seemed to have abnormally
large chests and their noses were similar to Jimmy
Durante's. They were grayish in appearance with bluish
lips and had very dark hair and eyes. She thought they
looked like mongoloids with their rounded faces and
broad foreheads. She described their eyes as being similar to those of cats; their skin was a bluish gray in

color. Mr. Hill states the men had a large cranium that got smaller in size toward the chin. He thought the eyes continued around to the sides of the heads, giving the impression that they had wider lateral vision than humans. The mouth was different than ours as it was long and thin like a horizontal line. The skin, he thought, was grayish and metallic looking but he did not notice if they had any hair and does not remember a large nose, just two slits in place of nostrils. Mrs. Hill stated that it was hard to look at these people but she thought the leader was different than the rest of the crew. The beings communicated by spoken language among themselves and talked with the Hills in English by means of telepathy. This is only one example of the many frightening experiences of contactees with saucerians.

The curious thing about several reported contacts with extraterrestrial beings is the fact that the contactee only remembers seeing the saucer. If the contactee is questioned thoroughly about the experience it can sometimes be shown that there is a time lapse in his story. There may be from thirty minutes to several hours of time unaccountable. The question as to what has taken place during this loss of time has led many contactees to submit to hypnosis. It is felt that the saucerians, having taken time to examine the various individuals, have then erased their memories of the whole experience with the exception of the fact that they saw a saucer.

A classic example of this type of contactee was an attorney from a small town in Wisconsin who claimed to have sighted a flying saucer. He was driving home after a business meeting that had lasted until midnight. He was extremely tired and admitted he had been drinking at dinner. According to his report he saw a flying object which looked like a bright light some twenty miles out of town. He thought it was a helicopter and continued watching it as it hovered over the highway ahead. When he passed under the object he noticed static on his radio and felt the interior of the car heat up. He also reported a severe headache and reached for aspirin which he had in the glove compartment. Continuing on his journey he turned off the highway onto an asphalt road heading toward his hometown when for some reason as yet unexplainable by him, he suddenly turned onto a dead-end gravel road which led to a swamp. There were no houses, lights, cars, or other people in this particular area, which is seldom visited.

As he drove over the crest of a hill he was amazed to see a flying saucer sitting in the middle of the road. Only quick reactions allowed him to stop the car without crashing into the saucer itself. The car stopped about fifteen feet from the saucer and he noticed a row of flickering bluish-green lights. Putting his car in reverse, his first thought was to get out of the area, when suddenly the engine stopped running, the headlights and dashlights went off, and his radio stopped playing. Admittedly the attorney was scared, realizing this was something far above his ability to cope. He saw some shadowy forms walking toward the car and feels he must have blacked out. What happened next was related after receiving psychiatric treatment with sessions under hypnosis. The attorney's only memory of the evening other than the story related above was one of seeing a bright light above the interstate highway and that the sun was coming up when he arrived home.

For several days he seemed unconcerned about the loss of time. He did report severe headaches. He became obsessed with politics and began to neglect his law practice in order to help in political campaigns. The attorney discovered a small wound like a welt on the back of his neck over his spinal cord. By midday it had become extremely painful and blistered. According to the doctor's examination there were many tiny perforations on the skin over the welt which had blistered by the afternoon of the day after contact. The following statements were made by the attorney under hypnosis.

He stated that his desire to enter politics was a foreign idea placed in his head by these visitors from another galaxy. Reportedly they came on the saucer he saw that night. He was told that they wanted a friend in politics so that when the time comes to reveal themselves to the world they will have friends in high places to prevent our people from killing them. Reportedly the saucerians were gathering specimens of rocks, weeds, trees, and dirt. He was told it was not uncommon to gather animals and people for their scientists to study. He felt assured that they meant him no harm and except for the welt and headaches, no harm came to him.

After this initial statement to the psychiatrist the attorney contacted a well-known author of books on UFOs who had written of several other similar contactee experiences in his books and magazine articles. After agreeing to use the case history under a pseudonym so as not to interfere with the attorney's law practice, further treatments under hypnosis were attempted.

In these sessions it was learned that the attorney was contacted by extraterrestrial beings after his car skidded to a stop before the saucer. Two individuals approached the car. Although he barely caught sight of them he stated the saucerian looked at him, then there was a blinding flash, and for some unknown reason the attorney opened the car door and stepped out. He was told they had to press something against his neck but that it would not hurt. Reportedly this was necessary to make communication possible. Some type of metallic device was pressed on the back of his neck and he stated he felt funny for a moment but admitted his fear, for some unknown reason, seemed to leave him. He was no longer confused and had the feeling that these people were his friends. He later reflected upon the experience that the use of this metallic device may in some way have inflicted a type of quick-acting tranquilizing drug that acts to calm the fears of human beings during saucer contact. He reported a pleasant feeling seemed to move throughout his whole body, similar to an experience he had in a hospital once after an injection of morphine.

The attorney saw five of these individuals and further stated he was invited inside their ship. He was questioned about our concept of time and reflects that for us to truly visit them or understand them we should learn to handle time correctly—more or less like a baby or child who has no concept of time. He states these people have visited our planet a number of times, perhaps in centuries past. As they approached the ship he estimated its size to be over one hundred feet in diameter. It was silver-gray in color and made out of some metal that looked like aluminum. The saucer rested on tripod legs that telescoped out of the bottom of the saucer. After a conversation between the captain of the ship and one of the individuals who seemed to be on guard, the attorney was escorted inside the saucer itself.

They entered by going up a ladder, which was extremely cold. He was taken into a large circular room and shown several screens where his picture was taken. His body temperature, brain waves, height, and weight were measured. He was apprehensive of his new surroundings inside the ship, which was cold and strange. He had a deep sense of fear that he might do something wrong and these people might harm him. Still he felt assured of their friendship. One interesting comment concerning the ship itself is that although it was made of metal he heard no sound from his walking upon it.

There were a lot of machines aboard the ship. The saucerians then gave him information as to how the ship was controlled. In their control room there were cases and discs made out of the same metal as the ship. Visibility to the outside was not handled by portholes or windows but by use of the screens.

He was asked if he was a rule maker. Apparently they found this interesting and it is thought by some experts that the saucerians are attempting to understand our legal structure. Later a cone-shaped object was placed upon his head; it made him feel as if his brain were being scrambled. It was the most painful thing he had ever experienced. He attempted to remove the object from his head, but they restrained him. When the pressure inside was finally released the thing was removed from his head. One of the saucerians grabbed him by the arm and squeezed it as if in reassurance.

Then he was taken out of the saucer and back to his car, where they told him they would meet again. As he sat in his car the saucerians returned to their ship, the ladder retracted, and the lights flickered. There was a buzzing and whirring sound as the saucer took off and disappeared into the heavens some thirty seconds later. Without any difficulty he started his engine, found that the lights and radio were operative, and went home.

Again, it is important for us to remember that the contact with the saucerians was not remembered except under hypnosis and that after returning home two or three hours later than he should have, he only remembers seeing an object in the sky. When home, he was too tired to even go to the bedroom. He lay on the couch and went to sleep. He reported a funny sound in his living room similar to a rattlesnake shaking his rattles or to the buzzing of bees. At this time he felt a strong desire to enter politics.

If such a visitation reported by a competent, reliable

attorney is to be believed and if this is not an uncommon experience, as experts tell us, then perhaps roaming the streets of our world, even in high places, there are several unknowing emissaries who have been contacted by these extraterrestrial visitors. Such a concept is shocking and yet a great many people believe it. According to this attorney the fact that he could be an agent programmed to run for office by some outside force is frightening. He still wonders how many other judges, lawyers, policemen, politicians, and others have had similar experiences and are now under their control.

Was his experience real? He certainly believes it was. Even when we realize the problem with hypnosis and delusion, the fact remains that these things can be accepted by the individual as reality. Even though there is no physical way of proving them wrong, one can still question it. The puzzling thing lies in the great number of these claims. If the visitation is not real, then there has to be an underlying explanation or phenomena which causes the individuals to believe it is real. This becomes the basic problem that we must solve if we are to understand the message and the meaning of these visitations.

If the attorney's testimony were to be taken by itself perhaps we could cast serious doubt on its reliability, but when we take into consideration the striking similarities between his story and others we must evaluate it in a different light. Take, for example, the case of a Nebraska policeman who was contacted by saucerians on December 3, 1967.

In this particular case the policeman was on routine patrol when he approached a highway intersection near the outskirts of town and saw a flying saucer. As in the previous case there was time missing in his official report; almost thirty minutes were unaccounted for. Again, he received a welt on the back of the neck above the spinal cord along with a tingling sensation. This particular case was reviewed by experts at the University of Colorado's headquarters for the Condon Committee investigating UFOs. It is reported in the official files of the Air Force's Project Blue Book. After several attempts to reconstruct the missing thirty minutes by the committee experts, the policeman also submitted himself to hypnosis in a private session after consulting with a leading expert in the field of UFOs. As in the previous case, a tremendous amount of information was provided by the officer about the working mechanisms of the flying saucer. Under hypnosis the report of his contact with the saucerians revealed a strong similarity to the attorney's report.

After entering the highway where he had been summoned to check on an accident, he reported the sighting of an object about two thirty in the morning. He assumed it was a truck with a flat tire and so he turned on his high beams to get a better look. There in front of him was a row of bright, flashing, red lights. The object in the distance left its resting place and continued up the hill. The officer followed. He attempted to call the station but found that his radio was dead. Next the engine in his vehicle cut out. He described the object as made of metal and shaped like a football with extremely bright lights with a silver glow around it and a flashing light underneath. It came over the field, hung there for a minute, lights flickering on and off, making some type of swishing sound. He estimated that the lights were flashing approximately one hundred twenty times a minute. The object lowered its three telescoping legs and landed.

Prevented from starting his vehicle and leaving, he reported that a being from inside the saucer approached his car. The officer thought about having his revolver ready but again stated that something in his mind prevented him from drawing it. The being in front of the car sprayed some type of gas or substance on the car itself. Then the saucerian pulled something out of a holster and the patrolman saw a bright flashing light, similar to the flash of a camera. The next thing he remembered after his eyes opened was rolling down the window and being touched by one of the beings on the side of the neck—the same place where the welt appeared later. He then opened the door and stepped outside the car. He was asked if he would like to enter the spaceship itself. He was told that the spaceship was propelled by some type of reversible electronic magnetism. This fact is interesting when we consider that electromagnetic receivers are being prepared to monitor saucer activity. He approached the ship with one of the saucerians, while another creature watched his cruiser. Walking underneath the craft, they entered the saucer through a circular opening by climbing up a telescoped ladder that was very cold.

He entered a big room inside the saucer where there were all kinds of gauges, boxes, and objects hanging from the ceiling. The room was about six feet high and twenty to twenty-six feet long. He reports there was a type of control panel off to one side with a wide screen above the console, tilted so as to be usable by an operator sitting at the panel. He could see out the portholes that ran around the ship. He noticed lots of tubes and pipes and some machinery with tapes on them which looked like computers. As the tapes ran, lights flickered on and off. The lighting inside the saucer gave off a reddish glow from some type of lighting strips on the ceiling.

He was told this was an observation craft and there were several others like it. They had been observing us for a long time and felt that if they slowly put out reports, making contacts with those who would tell the truth, it would help them present their case to mankind. They want to confuse people because they are being sighted too often but they hope to have people believe in them when the invasion starts. He was sure the word "invasion" meant an open showing of themselves and not declared warfare. The officer is sure they are not hostile.

Reportedly the visitors are from a nearby galaxy. They have bases on Venus and some of the other planets in our galaxy. There were many other details given concerning the flight capabilities of the saucer.

The saucerians said that the people of earth were attempting to do things in the wrong way, but they did not provide any information as to what the right way would be. The police officer was not to tell that he had been on a ship. He feels he was programmed to state only that he saw a craft landing below the intersection of the highway, that he approached it, that it shot up into the air. They plan to return and see him two more times. He was told that he would be approached by one of his own people and that he would know him when he came.

Again the saucerian placed a hand on his shoulder, led him out of the saucer, back to his vehicle. The saucerians climbed back into their ship and made motions for him to return to his car. The legs of the saucer retracted, a reddish orange light came out of the bottom of the ship, and then the saucer moved upward into the sky. He described it as looking like a shooting star because of the speed with which it disappeared into the night sky.

He states that the saucer was exactly one hundred and two feet in diameter and stood about thirty-five feet off the ground. With the tripods retracted the ship was about twenty feet high. According to the saucerians, the officer was contacted by accident and just happened to be there at the wrong time. A great deal of technical information about the saucerians and the saucer itself was provided to him and one wonders if we can accept all of it as true. It is interesting that even the author to whom the above information was given leaves the question open as to the validity of the contactee's claims. Either someone is trying to confuse us totally by an extensive campaign or the story the contactee gives is true and we are being prepared for a mass contact or, as they put it, an invasion in the future.

The striking similarities between these and, according to experts, the hundreds of other accounts like them make them difficult to explain away. In general, the UFO is sighted on the ground or hovering close to the ground. It is often accompanied by a sound of buzzing or humming similar to that of a swarm of bees. There is an amount of time which is unaccounted for— the contactee in some cases loses several hours. In many cases the contactee begins a crusade to tell people of the friendly message of the saucerians. In this respect the life of the contactee has been drastically changed and he takes on a new missionary fervor to proclaim the message of the saucerians. He is often plagued with headaches and restlessness. He finds it difficult to sleep and, as would be expected, he has nightmares and dreams about his experience. He has tremendous suffering from the physical torment he has been through.

It is fascinating to note that the contactee in general has had no previous experience with flying saucers and, for that matter, no previous interest. After the initial shock and fear of the visitation the contactee no longer seems to fear these visitors and seems to look forward to their return.

Perhaps the most fascinating comment made by experts concerning the ordeal of a contactee has to do with his reactions and mannerisms of speech while he is relating his story under hypnosis. The response seems robot-like and comes from a deep voice seemingly within the individual. In general, it is not the normal voice of the individual. Even after the individual is told to remember these things after hypnosis, he still maintains the automatic response and the deep voice within. It has been observed in many cases that as questions about the ordeal are answered by the contactee he may pause for several seconds (or, in some cases, for half a minute) before giving his answer. Again it seems to be an automatic response, not in his normal speaking voice. Even his manner changes. The contactee seems to be controlled or, in the more ancient use of the word, possessed.

In order to gain a further understanding of the meaning of these visitations by extraterrestrial beings, to discover why people are being contacted, and even to explain the nature of this control, it seems inevitable that we turn our attention next to the saucerians themselves in order to fully understand the reality of their message.

THREE

The Claims

With the numerous books now available on the subject of UFOs, it becomes increasingly more difficult to actually pinpoint the identity of the saucerians. Some believe they are inhabitants of far distant galaxies. Others believe we are being visited by several different groups. And there are others who feel that these are demons or devils, while still more proclaim that they have been visited by angels. There is an increasingly large body of believers in the new religion of UFOlogy who feel the saucerians fulfill, and for that matter have helped to establish, Biblical prophecy and miracles. There is also a strong body of belief in the premise that these visitors are our gods returning to visit us again. It is hard to imagine all of these possibilities being true. Although much research has been done by various experts in the field, there is still a great deal of disagreement and at present the identity of the saucerians still remains a mystery.

It is the purpose of this chapter to examine some of the various claims in order to place these sightings into a proper perspective so the mystery may be solved. No one really knows if these experiences are real, but they seem real enough to the people experiencing them. These frightening and sometimes terrifying events have lodged themselves in the conscious and unconscious mind of the contactee and he definitely feels he has been visited by saucerians.

Perhaps the most perplexing problem facing us in understanding the identity of the saucerians lies in the distinct differences of the beings themselves, as reported by contactees. In Mississippi two shipyard workers claim they were taken aboard a UFO and examined by crab-clawed creatures. It is interesting that they remember the experience and that under a lie detector test and hypnosis they repeated the same tale. Of course, we would not expect creatures from outer space to be monstrous unless we are talking about science fiction. Still, experts insist that we can judge these creatures by our own experience and that the many mysteries that face us in our own world should open our eyes to the fact that strange things do occur. After all, there is a wide difference between bacteria and man, plants and animals, vertebrates and invertebrates. Jellyfish are certainly much different from humans. Who is to say we really understand and comprehend why people are dominant on this planet? After all, the evolutionary explanation would require that human beings dominate merely by chance development. Considering that most proponents of the existence of extraterrestrial life base that existence on evolutionary development, it seems logical to them that any type of creature could develop intelligence and be the dominant force on the planet, in the solar system, or in the galaxy. As strange as this may seem, there are many claims from contactees of abduction by monstrous creatures; but this is not the ordinary saucerian. Nor is the occasional sighting of little green men a requirement for belief in saucerians for, although on rare occasions small men are sighted, the normal claim by those who have been contacted by extraterrestrial visitors is that the people look very much like ourselves.

A Dallas salesman stopped on the road and planned to sleep for a few hours before continuing his journey home. Because of the value of the merchandise he carried on his trips he was armed with a small pistol, which he kept under the dashboard. Locking the doors, he settled down for a nap only to awaken suddenly after a few minutes of sleep feeling that something was wrong. Sitting up he found there were no other cars in the area. He turned and looked directly into the face of a man with a long beard and dressed in a monk's robe. The hood was pulled up around his head and the salesman reports he was quite visible as the rest area was quite well lit. Something prevented him, he says, from reaching for his pistol. They stared at each other a few moments and the strange visitor turned and walked toward a grove of trees. Just before he reached the trees the man disappeared. Experts say that this is a common occurrence, that bearded individuals in monk's clothing with caps and hoods have been seen all over the world. These people are reported to vanish or disappear without any evidence of their existence. If such an occurrence took place near a graveyard, one might consider them ghosts.

The sighting of an individual who suddenly appears and disappears, possibly walking through walls or other solid objects, accompanied by weird glowing lights that seem to float in the room itself often accompany UFO activity. There seems to be a strange connection between these bearded figures and UFO contact. In some instances television reception has been interrupted and a bearded monkish figure may speak to the people or only to one individual in the room. There have been several instances similar to this which have been reported. The message seems to indicate a warning to individuals to help solve the problems of the world. One farmer was asked to write the government to tell them to stop testing atomic weapons because there was too much radioactivity in the air. He was told to stop using DDT because of the pollution to rivers and oceans. He was told that someone would contact him. The interesting thing about the report is that the being spoke in clear, distinct English and sounded just like one of the neighbors. Several people who claim to have seen a UFO also have experienced visitations in their homes.

The phenomena of invisible powers and sudden appearances of strange beings has been reported down through the ages and, of course, have their place in legends and even in religious observances in many lands. Some experts in the field of extraterrestrial visitation and UFOs feel this is a strong indication that our

planet has been visited for a long time. As remarkable
as these claims are they seem somewhat tame when we
consider the reports of the policeman and the attorney
mentioned in the previous chapter.

In the case of the attorney, the inhabitants of the
flying saucer that contacted him and took him inside
for a visit were normal in their appearance. They did
not appear and disappear suddenly but seemed to be
real, perhaps giving credence to the concept of extraterrestrial visitation. They spent time gathering specimens to study and seemed interested in the exchange of
ideas and concepts, attempting to converse concerning
our understanding of time and the universe. Although
they seemed to have a plan there were no specific
warnings of judgment or doom. The impression was
given that they were preparing to reveal themselves in
the future and were contacting individuals with the idea
of preparing for that visitation. They have a high technology, as evidenced by the many devices they carry
which evidently allow them to manipulate the mind.
They have the ability to cause a false sense of euphoria
and seem to be able to control the individuals they
contact.

The attorney reported that the captain of the ship
was approximately five and a half feet tall. He was
dressed in a white uniform much like coveralls; he
wore a black belt with a silver-gray box on the side.
The attorney was told that the box in some way helped
in the communication process. According to the attorney's testimony, the other saucerians were a little over
five feet tall and weighed under one hundred and fifty
pounds. They appeared to be in good physical condition, but this was hard to determine since their uniforms completely covered their bodies. Their faces
were smaller than ours but this particular observation
could be due to the type of head covering they wore.
Their eyes were reportedly slanted with thin-lined eye-

brows slanted over heavy-lidded eyes. Their skin was lightly colored and was reminiscent of ancient Egyptian gods although not as dark. They had thin lips which are said to be the same color as their facial skin.

It is reported that they have developed a type of travel that in some way overcomes the force of gravity. They described it as a type of push-pull mechanism that uses the earth's gravity to push them out into space. Once free of our gravitational system, they lock onto another planet or object to propel or pull them on. All of this is fully automatic and is evidently accomplished by one of the computer-like machines which the attorney saw in the vehicle. Travel on a particular planet was accomplished by some type of electromagnetic force which is utilized to drive the saucer. He was told that our people are very close to developing a similar device. The use of atomic energy as a source of power for space flight was described as not suitable because of the dangers of being out in space with this type of engine. Reportedly they had lost many individuals in their experiments with this particular power source. On their home planet they use water for energy. The attorney was told that we should be doing experiments to learn and understand the use of this powerful energy force by breaking water down to its ultimate form of matter. This may explain why many saucers are sighted over lakes and streams and why some observers have the impression that moisture or water is being taken into the saucer.

The attorney was told by the saucerian that they have ships capable of traveling with the speed of light squared, but they abandoned them because of the problems they caused. Traveling at these speeds caused the creatures' bodies to disintegrate into particles of matter, thus making it necessary for a machine to be developed to reassemble them upon arrival. Unfortunately they found it difficult to reassemble the individuals and reported that some of them came back as monsters. A second problem developed as some of the saucerians decided to stay in the pure energy form, thus giving them the freedom to go whenever and wherever they wanted simply by thinking themselves there. Because they were pure energy the entire universe was open to them. This allowed them to enter other beings, plants, animals, or even solid rock as they pleased. He was also told that a similar device was used when the saucer enters our atmosphere, causing it to be invisible. This may explain the great difficulty in picking them up by radar, since they possess the ability to disappear at will. Supposedly our communication systems are being monitored and because of their intricate security system they are able to tell when they are about to be spotted or when a jet is sent to investigate and thus they simply make themselves invisible.

The attorney got the distinct impression that this particular crew was military in purpose and was sent to observe our planet for scientific purposes. Reportedly earth people are extremely hostile and apparently there has been difficulty in the past; crews have been missing or harmed since, according to the saucerian, they are not immortal.

As stated earlier they seem interested in our system of law and order and evidently recorded all they needed to know in the attorney's mind when the device was placed on his head. They had the ability of brain manipulation and quite possibly had recorded the conscience, subconscience, and memory banks of each individual they contacted. They seemed friendly and interested in the activities of the inhabitants of the planet Earth and for some reason we seem to fit into their plans.

The similarities between the individuals sighted by the attorney and by the policeman are so remarkable that it is hard to imagine how two individuals in different parts of the country over a three-year span could have had the same experience. In the policeman's report he states that the eyes of the individuals were very similar to cat's eyes, that although he did not like to look directly into them, he found he could not look away. The eyes did not blink. The saucerians do not wear any type of breathing apparatus but are evidently able to breath normally in our atmosphere. In fact, he did not notice them breathing at all. He reported that they communicated by voice and by telepathy. It appeared to him that all speaking was done through an antenna device over the ear area of the helmet. He reports the voice spoke in broken English. It was a strange sound and appeared to come from deep inside the being, not from the mouth. He was told that they had studied our language with the help of some type of machine. Somehow he was given the impression that they could speak any language on earth wherever they landed.

In commenting on the guards, he said they appeared to walk very stiffly and straight like soldiers. Their heads moved back and forth. They wore silver uniforms which were very shiny and looked like metal. They wore boots of silver but no sound was made on the metal when they walked. He stated that they were from four and a half to five feet in height. They wore a belt that was also made of the silver-gray metal with a highly polished buckle. He reported that the uniforms were designed like coveralls. The helmet seemed to be part of the uniform itself. He did not notice any zippers, buttons, or other fasteners. The ears were covered and seemed to be the thickest part of the helmet section of the uniform. There was an antenna which came out of the right side over the ear.

Again, he reports that the heads were thinner and elongated and were not formed like a human skull. They had large chests and seemed extremely muscular.

He described them as being military because of their good posture. He described the eyes in the same manner as did the attorney, with a thin eyebrow slanted upward. The eyes themselves were definitely those of the Oriental. They had flat noses and thin lips which made their mouths look more like slits. Again, he mentioned that the color of the lips was the same as the color of the skin. It was the eyes that impressed him the most, cat's eyes with a pupil that became more like a long slant going up and down rather than round like ours.

He perceived the tallest individual to be close to five and a half feet, a fact which makes the similarity between the two accounts more striking. He thought they were about thirty years old. He did not notice any conversation between the individuals and felt that if they did so it must be through the antenna device.

From his contact he learned that the ship was made of 100 percent magnesium. He noticed it was very polished and the surface was smooth; when touching it he could not find any rough spots. The speed of the craft was given to him as over one-hundred and fifty thousand miles per hour.

He was told that they carry weapons, some type of ray gun which is not intended to kill but to paralyze. He did not notice any other type of armaments on the ship itself. He was asked about a specific reservoir and was told they pick up water and drain a type of power from it. As scientists, he was told that they pick up animals and some people to use in experiments. He believes that many of these people have been released with their brains manipulated and have become agents in our world.

Inside the saucer itself he was shown various equipment. One device was a small saucer-shaped object, five to six feet in diameter, which was used for observation. It was constructed of the same metal as the saucer but there were no openings or antenna visible.

This particular disc is used for surveillance of an area which may explain why saucers can find remote areas to land, fairly secure in the fact that no humans are nearby. He was told that this device was developed because of the hostile people who had bothered them in the past and therefore it was necessary to scan an area before landing. Pictures are taken by the baby saucer and relayed back to the parent ship in a very elaborate system. Both pictures and sound are transmitted back to the saucer. He was told that only on rare occasions do they land in an area where human activity is found. Normally they attempt to avoid this.

He was shown pictures through a large screen above what appeared to be a console on one side of the saucer. Although he does not remember if the pictures were colored or not, he does state they were vivid and real like a 3-D movie and not like any we have seen. While on board they switched the screen to someplace overhead and picked up three saucers flying in formation from very far away. He was told that this visible picture was accomplished by some type of light beam. He was also informed that some of their craft had highly powerful devices in the form of light beams that can allow them to scan a house or building anywhere in the world. He says this particular type of saucer stayed high in the atmosphere moderating their activities in various places of the world. He was also shown a picture of a large craft that was high above the earth in outer space. He was told that this was headquarters or what we refer to as a mother ship. This larger vehicle was used to fly between planets carrying with it a lot of observation craft and that the flying saucer he was on was assigned to their base here on earth.

Reportedly they have bases all over our planet. An underwater base is reported off the coast of Florida in the region known as the Bermuda Triangle. It is interesting to note that this particular area is infamous for the lost ships and planes that have vanished mysteriously in the past few hundred years. There is another underwater base off the coast of Argentina. He was told there were two bases in the United States, and one in the polar region. They also have bases on Venus and other planets.

Apparently the saucerians defend themselves by creating a force field, which accounts for their ability to stop car engines and silence radio communications when they feel it is necessary. Because of their defense mechanisms he felt it would be impossible to burst into one of their saucers, but he was told that bullets can stop a saucerian. Fear of injury, therefore, explains the high degree of secrecy and mystery surrounding their investigations. He also reported that the saucer had a built-in destruct mechanism which the mother ship could use to destroy an observation ship without a trace before it reached the ground. This is done only if there is some mechanical failure that might allow the ship to be captured. The saucerians stated that we were being observed by creatures from other parts of the galaxy who know more about us than they do. This, then, may account for other types of saucers and sightings by various individuals. Although there was no lettering, insignias, or markings on any of the ships, the patrolman did mention an insignia worn on the left side of the uniform. This insignia, according to his description, looked like a snake with wings. Although much speculation has been made concerning this particular insignia, let it be stated that the winged serpent or flying serpent has played a great role in the legends and traditions of Central and South America. When asked to draw a picture of the emblem, he drew a feathered serpent with wings. The significance of this emblem and the many sightings of people and beings with the winged serpent on their chest and the use of the winged serpent in folklore certainly may be a key in learning their identity. Some people have even suggested that it may be significant of the story of Adam and Eve on our own planet, considering the role of the serpent there.

These two cases, of the attorney and policeman, are similar to literally hundreds of reported contacts with saucerians. There is the famous story of George Adamski, who claims to have been taken by saucerians to the planet Venus. He reports contact with the Venusian spaceman Orthon. There are, of course, many other reported contacts, some visual and some merely with voices. One group in San Diego, California, is now reportedly receiving messages from famous scientists such as Einstein and others whose beings now live in the distant confines of our galaxy. Reportedly new scientific information is being transmitted to us from these new visitors to outer space.

At any rate, there is great mystery involved in understanding the identity of the saucerians. There seem to be many different types and before we can truly venture an opinion as to their purpose and plan for the planet Earth, it seems inevitable that we first discuss their message. The real meaning of these visitations and, of course, the basic question considering the future of mankind, since more contact with these saucerians seems evident, can only be answered as we evaluate the message that they have for the inhabitants of planet Earth.

FOUR

The Message

With the advent of the scientific age of technology there are many unexplained phenomena which occur all around us. Because of man's resistance to the acceptance by faith of the unexplained, he constantly seeks out answers in order to understand that which is beyond his comprehension. The concept of God certainly falls into the category of the unexplainable and admittedly requires faith on the part of the believer to accept the fact that God exists. But history has proved that this is a reasonable faith; yet man continually attempts to explain God and the mysteries of His universe.

In our age of technology it is now concluded by many millions of people that God does not exist. With his freedom of choice man has ignored God and chosen to worship technology or intelligence or his own achievements, placing these above the worship of the Creator as Paul so clearly warned in the first chapter of Romans. It is not the lack of evidence that causes man to accept this position but simply his inability to believe God and try Him by faith. This may explain why the premise of extraterrestrial visitors to our planet in the past is gaining such wide acceptance among thousands of people. Man was created with an inward void that can only be filled by faith in God. This new concept of UFOlogy explains God in terms that man can now comprehend. God is no longer the almighty, all-powerful Creator of the universe, but simply an intelligent supertechnological being who evolved to his present state on some remote planet in a far distant galaxy long before man ever came into existence on this planet.

Little does man realize that it takes a greater faith to believe in a supertechnological being without understanding where that being came from than it does to believe in an all-powerful, supernatural Creator whose existence needs no explanation. For naturally a God

who has the power to call by the power of the spoken
Word the heavens and the earth into existence does not
need an explanation concerning His origin for His
power dictates His authority. Still man finds it easier to
believe in things which he can explain and so we are
faced with a new challenge to the power and authority
of the almighty God of the Bible. He is claimed to be a
visitor from outer space who travels in a flying saucer
to various planets throughout the galaxy. Although we
do not understand where he came from, he is said to
have many followers who also travel in flying saucers.
These beings have appeared to man throughout history
and have made man what he is today. Even now,
somewhere on this planet, a man is being visited by one
of these extraterrestrial creatures, receiving his instructions for the future visitation of God here on this planet. It is supposedly said that belief in these creatures
requires a rejection of the supernatural God of the
Bible, yet their message is in many ways identical to
the Biblical prophecies presented in the book of Revelation.

But why is their message so similar? What is the
purpose of their predictions? In order to answer these
questions and understand this new threat to Christianity it becomes necessary to evaluate the messages of
these visitors in order to gain insight into their meanings.

These visitors from outer space in many instances
claim to be angels sent to prepare the way for the coming of Christ. They warn us of great disasters which are
before us on the horizon. They prophesy doom and yet
promise peace if we will listen and obey their message.
In many instances they talk of a creator although sur-
prisingly they do not refer to God as the word express-
ing this creator. We are told that as earthlings we really
know very little about this creator, that our understanding is shallow; the saucerians' knowledge is much

broader. Their message would indicate that they strictly adhere to the laws of the creator instead of to the laws of materialism that are so prevalent in the dominion of man. Those who have talked with these visitors are led to believe in many instances that the saucerians live according to the will of the creator and not by their own personal will.

In some instances the beings claim to be from planets within our own solar system and in others they claim to come from far beyond our own galaxy, from planets we know nothing about. Supposedly many earth people have willingly been kidnapped and are now living on other planets.

One advocate of UFOlogy, considered by many to be the earth's foremost ambassador to outer space, believes there are many extraterrestrial beings walking our streets now in order to carry out their sacred message here on the planet Earth. He states they are far ahead of us in their technology and in their relation to the cosmos. But he also states that these visitors are cautious because they wish to avoid crucifixion. It is his belief that one can be contacted by one of our space brothers if one can only learn to blend his soul consciousness with the cosmic consciousness. However, this must be done by faith, for without faith truth will never be known. He believes that the mind that has no faith will never know true life and happiness, that consciousness is the parent of all things including the mind. When the mortal mind tries to operate only on behalf of itself it is opposing the special consciousness. He believes that anyone who wishes to help in this cause will have to learn to blend his soul consciousness with the all-encompassing soul of the cosmos; then he may recognize these space brothers when they meet. He further states that many earthlings have already met these people unknowingly.

The universal language is reported to be a language

of telepathy. He feels this telepathy is the invisible feeling impulses that are the cosmic consciousness flowing as a cosmic force through all manifestation. It is through mental telepathy that we will know and understand the great message of the saucerians. He feels that through this type of communication one day all artificial barriers that separate people, whether it is race, creed, color, or simply a problem of pride and vanity, will eventually be overcome and people will be united with themselves and with nature. He believes that this is the one language which every atom in the universe is able to speak and understand. In essence, then, he is saying that by faith we can learn and know all things and eventually communicate with all beings, merging our consciousness with the very atoms of the universe. We learn this by controlling our emotions, becoming self-disciplined, because it is the control of the senses that is the key to contact with these beings from outer space.

These are the claims of George Adamski who, before his death in 1965, had written numerous books on contact with extraterrestrial visitors. He claims to have visited the planet Venus with the being Orthon, whom he described as a being very much like ourselves—approximately five and one-quarter feet tall, weighing one hundred and thirty-five pounds, and approximately thirty years of age. He claimed to have taken several trips into outer space and talked about the fireflies he saw during his trip. This fact is fascinating since he mentions these long before they were reported by the United States and Russian astronauts venturing into those unknown regions.

As adamant as he was concerning the possibility of contact with the saucerians, he stated before his death that of the three thousand claims by contactees of communication with the space brothers only eight hundred had been genuine. An editor of a widely read science fiction magazine states that Adamski's story was originally submitted to him in manuscript form and talked of the coming of Jesus Christ in a flying saucer. This editor states that the manuscript was rejected because of its controversial nature. He goes on to mention that after reading Adamski's book that the person of Jesus Christ was changed to the being Orthon, a visitor from Venus, and that essentially the story and content were the same as the manuscript he had previously rejected.

Adamski's claims are filled with thoughts about God the Divine Father who is in charge of all beings. He continually talks about the sayings of Christ and feels that he is doing His work, that he has been chosen and called into special service to proclaim a new message on this earth.

He admits to attending meetings comprised of people from Mars, Venus, Saturn, Jupiter, Uranus, and Neptune. These meetings were just friendly get-togethers to discuss the everyday problems of life. At these meetings he learned about the eating habits of saucerians. They eat fish at about the same ratio most of us eat meat, while their meat eating is comparable to the average earthling's consumption of fish. Having studied our food supplies carefully they find that they are healthier if they eat meat once or twice a week while they are here. According to Adamski they usually purchase the cheaper cuts of meat which can be boiled with vegetables. They are very fond of all vegetables and make appetizing soups from beans, potatoes, and other vegetables. And they naturally like raw fruits and vegetables prepared as salads. What Adamski is saying is that these people are very much like those on our planet, not fanatics. He cautions us with the words of Jesus that one should not worry about what goes into the mouth but what comes out (Matt. 15:11). Adamski's comments are very different from those of many other contactees. He places a strong emphasis on learning and understanding the Creator.

Not all claims of saucer visitation are as controversial as those of Adamski. There are many instances of visitation that as yet seem hard to explain. Interwoven in the message is the promise of peace and brotherhood as we are assured of the friendliness of the saucerians. There is always a definite warning to give up our continuing exploration for materialistic gains. Naturally we are asked to trust the saucerians, to learn to rely on them, to have faith in their message and promise of peace. In many instances we are asked to lay aside our atomic weapons in order to prepare for the world to come.

In some cases the contactee hears only a voice within his consciousness. The voice carries a warning of impending disasters but promises peace through the use of its supernatural power if we will only believe and heed the warning. The contactee is told that in some way he is to help save the world. He must, with missionary fervor, proclaim the message of the saucerians. In this type of case the contactee is likened to a mental patient inflicted with schizophrenia. Experts refer to this type of contactee as a case of UFO possession— the earthling seems to be in the control of an entity from outer space.

One leading expert states that he has talked with several cases of contactees whom he feels have been possessed by UFO entities. In many of the cases they even claim contact with the same being, Ashtar, whom he describes as a "mental flimflam man." Ashtar claims to be from the planet Mars, the star Orion, star constellations beyond our galaxy, and from another dimension as well. In one instance this expert spells out in detail, Ashtar contacted a Missouri businessman. Considered a "cosmic conman," Ashtar attempts to gain the confidence of the contactee by revealing the past and predicting the future.

This particular businessman stated that he was not concerned with flying saucers and even went so far as to state that people who reported flying saucers were possibly touched in the head. After a business meeting he was driving home and had a flat tire. This happened on a deserted stretch of road. When he opened his trunk he found the spare tire was flat also. He left the car and began the two-mile walk to his home. On his way he noticed a small light one foot in diameter in a field off to his left. He says it was not a bright light but a misty light. He stopped to look at it for a few moments because it seemed out of place. As he continued home he noticed the light seemed to be following him. When he stopped, the light stopped. When he noticed this, fear broke out and he began to run. The light kept pace. He was so concerned with the small light that reportedly he did not pay attention to what was happening behind him. After hearing a faint buzzing sound which he described as a high pitched whine, he turned and saw a flying saucer about twenty feet off the ground. Fear engulfed him and he stood still, protecting his eyes from the brightest red light he ever saw. The large saucer did not move but, as he stood there, the small misty light went over his head and entered into the larger saucer which quickly disappeared into the night sky. Not knowing what to do he rapidly walked to his home and naturally, because of what people might say, did not discuss the incident with anyone.

Seven days later he reports that a voice came to him as he was lying in bed attempting to go to sleep. He reported a heavy throbbing in his head and took aspirin to rid himself of the headache. When he heard the voice it appeared to be coming from within his mind. At first he thought his mind was playing tricks on him but has since come to the conclusion that the experience was real. The businessman came in contact with Ashtar, who reported himself to be a member of the United Council of the Universal Brotherhood, the elders that govern the universe. He was told that they needed his help in order to prevent the earth from being destroyed. He felt a terrible pain in his head but was assured it would stop.

Communication was handled through telepathy, which Ashtar reported was possible through some type of electronic, brain-wave vibrating machine on board his spacecraft high in the atmosphere above the businessman's house. He was told of the advanced technology and superiority of the saucerians. He was promised business skills that would make him extremely wealthy because, according to Ashtar, they need people of wealth to proclaim their message. When asked for proof that Ashtar was who he said he was, he was told of events from his childhood. After several hours of conversation with a voice within his mind, the conversation ended and Ashtar was gone.

The same experience occurred several times over a period of several months, during which time Ashtar accurately predicted the headlines in newspapers and gave the businessman tips on the stock market. The man became convinced that Ashtar was real and believed his claim that he was a being from outer space. Ashtar commanded him to become a preacher and was instructed to go forth and teach the world, starting a new church in order to save humanity. He was told that he was to become the new messiah with the power to heal and the ability to attract millions of people because he would have the gift to-help others. The businessman refused but feels he would have helped had they given him something to do within his own ability. He did not feel he was capable of becoming a messiah.

By his own admission he was not a deeply religious man.

Ashtar began to threaten him with his powers in order to convince him of the need for this missionary venture. During the experience his business had been neglected and his wife was filing for divorce. Reportedly he became sloppy and careless in his dress and appearance and he became more philosophical in his thinking rather than bothering with mundane things like shaving. He began to see a psychologist and was told that possibly he possessed a manifestation of a schizoid personality. Treatment did not help but it angered Ashtar. He was forbidden to go to the doctor and instead Ashtar promised him a tip on the stock market. He was told he would become wealthy beyond his wildest dreams. He put fifty thousand dollars in some stock. In a matter of weeks he had lost thirty-seven thousand dollars of his investment. Ashtar was gone.

After that things returned to normal but the businessman reports that he handles his affairs much differently now. He is more congenial and would not drive his competitors out of business, as he had done before the visitation occurred. He states that he was shown the entire universe and reportedly saw the wonders of the heavens. Again, he believes the experience was real. It is interesting that Ashtar claimed to be like the angels mentioned in the Bible, a messenger sent down to help us. The most perplexing problem to the businessman who refused to follow Ashtar's instructions concerns the question of what he would have gained had he followed the orders of the saucerian.

Not all mental contactees have had the same good fortune of escape as the Missouri businessman. One individual accepted the challenge with a missionary-like zeal. She went to Washington, D.C., to fulfill the mission presented to her by a saucerian from Jupiter. She was to obtain an official investigation into flying saucers as well as receive comments from government officials on a flying saucer design supplied by her visitors. Her mission was a complete failure. Perhaps upset by this failure or else in a sincere effort to gain the government recognition she desired for her project, she locked herself in her hotel room and started a fast for peace. Sixty-six days later, without hearing from the government or receiving any further message from her contact from Jupiter, she died at the age of thirty-seven. It is hard to understand that if these messengers are truly angels from heaven why this contactee was required to give her life without any further reassurance or hope from her saucerian.

Ashtar, along with other entities from space such as Monka and Mohanda, have provided us with several messages to help us in our understanding of saucer people. Although there is much disagreement concerning the necessity of accepting these messages by advocates of UFOlogy, many such as Adamski reject the messages of Ashtar as false, containing only a fraction of the truth. It seems important to our understanding of the problem that we examine what these beings are saying.

The Ashtar Commands list nine guidelines for attempting space contacts.

1. We are not to attempt to contact space people for they can contact us at any time in any form they choose, depending on the level of advancement of their evolution.

2. We are to prepare ourselves spiritually for some type of work. This does not mean a type of religious practice but instead one is to look within one's self for these higher spiritual qualities. We are also told that we must help others around us to find this same peace and inner joy.

3. We are to live each day in service to the Creator
    for we are known by the saucerians by our work.
    They are able to judge our aura and thereby know
    if we are truly worthy of being a part of the
    mighty work of the saucerians upon this planet.
    From this aura they learn of our past but it also
    indicates what we will be able to accomplish spirit-
    ually.

4. We are instructed to live each day as if it were our
    last, therefore we are not to look back or live in
    the past but instead are instructed to place all of
    our dreams and desires into the service of God
    and man.

5. We are warned against negative attitudes because
    they breed fear and doubt, leaving us confused
    and ignorant. It is our spiritual understanding that
    is the key to all UFO activity. The saucerians offer
    spiritual guidance to those who sincerely seek.

6. We are warned that earth is to be a battleground
    and here the forces of evil employ ships of great
    size and beauty just as the forces of good do.
    Earthlings who are unprepared are warned not to
    seek contact with the saucerians unless they find
    out how to put a positive force field around them.
    Negative or evil forces can and do abduct thou-
    sands of people from the earth each year.

7. We are to establish a contact with our godhead for
    no power on earth or even outside can harm a per-
    son who is dwelling in perfect accord with his
    higher self. Such contact is available to any who
    choose it. The finding of one's higher self is the
    most important thing in life.

8. We are to establish contact by meditation and con-
    centration because these bring awareness. We are
    instructed to be in the world but not of the world

by giving up fleshly pursuits. By meditation upon perfection we will gain a victory over evil, sickness, and ignorance, thereby gaining an understanding of God. We are to concentrate on gaining a balance, for service to the saucerians is impossible if we are in an unbalanced condition.

9. We are instructed that the kingdom of God is built by light and meditation. We must think about it in order to attract saucerians who, according to Ashtar, are creatures of light. We are to seek and demand truth and it shall be given to us. This is said to be a universal law and by understanding this we show wisdom. We are told that we are spirit and this is what is important. We must realize, regardless of what form we are in now, that we must learn to know ourselves and to be true to our inner knowledge, which is the greatest key to gaining contact with the saucerians. This is to bring the kingdom of heaven within us, thus enabling us to express the kinship of God.

It is hard to understand the true meaning and purpose of Ashtar's claims and advocates of UFOlogy still wonder at the meaning of his messages. We are told that by knowing ourselves we will know the Creator. Such a concept is so drastically different than the Biblical premise of commitment to the law of God through the ministry of the Holy Spirit that obviously we must seriously question the claims of Ashtar. It is interesting to note that prominent theologians and ministers are lending their support to the concept that these are messengers from God. Leading churchmen everywhere are attempting to understand the UFO phenomenon and many believe it has great significance in our understanding of future events for the planet Earth. There is widespread controversy as to the purpose and intent of these individuals, but it is definitely felt that they are in some way connected to judgment that is prophesied in the Bible.

The Bible claims that God will take His people out of this world before judgment occurs. This event is known as the rapture. Could this extraterrestrial visitation by beings that claim to be angels be in some way connected with this event? One noted authority in the field states that the UFOs are piloted by God's angels who are right now preparing to take God's people safely out of this world to abide on other planets before the final judgment and destruction of the world in which we live. It is certain that the Bible has a great deal to say about beings that are higher than man and perhaps this lends support to the concept. But before a final determination concerning the visits of the saucerians is reached let us examine their message in more detail.

A Canadian girl claims to have been contacted by an individual named Oh-Ho who warned of judgment to come but assured her she would be taken off the planet first. According to Oh-Ho the earth was to crystallize but she would be safe if she thought of the disasters in a spiritual manner. She was instructed that God saves those who want to be saved. He predicted a series of cataclysmic disasters that, though temporary in nature, would completely change the structure of the world. She was told to read the book of Revelation to obtain a description of the coming disasters. He predicted widespread panic, which of course would be expected in the light of what was happening. He warned her to stay away from large cities. He seemed to refer to this time period as the "ultimate last day" and stated that it must happen to every individual. He predicted there would be no place to hide but instructed her to be proud for humans are taking a great new step, a step which the saucerians or space brothers have already taken.

He talked of the long time it takes to evolve to the point to which it is said we are now. He told her to be searching for the truth, never hide from it but hunt for it, seek it wherever she was. She was instructed to be concerned for her fellow beings and help them whenever possible.

In addition, Oh-Ho predicted the return of Jesus Christ whom he referred to as "Esu." Reportedly He will return near water because water is His sign. He is to return where His own people are gathered and we are to know Him even though He is different from what would be expected. We are to know Him by His eyes which, according to Oh-Ho, we have seen before. His return was predicted in an area close to the Great Lakes. After the judgment and disaster this area will be changed, being more tropical in nature and it will be known at that time as the Western Lakes.

Oh-Ho predicted other disasters, such as the tilting of the earth's axis which will cause a physical destruction of the earth as it now exists. Only a few things will survive this final destruction and followers of God will be taken away where they will be safe. This final destruction will prepare for the crystallization of the earth, after which those followers who were taken to other planets during this destruction will return to find a new earth. It is his prediction that the true believers of God will be taken to other worlds during this judgment and will return after the judgment has taken place.

In addition to this prediction, many other specific judgments were mentioned as he talked about various parts of the earth that are in danger of sinking into the ocean or being destroyed by earthquakes. Although it seems to be commonplace among contactees to predict disasters, the concept of people who believe in God being taken to other planets where they will survive in peace and then be brought back to this earth to live in a new paradise is certainly fascinating. When we consider that saucerians are not the only people who predict the earth is coming to an end we begin to ask the all-important, universal question: "Are we to believe the claims of these saucerians?"

For years now occultists and psychics have been predicting doom and destruction as eminent on the planet Earth. Although the cataclysms they predict will take place will affect literally millions of people, there seems to be little interest or concern. In January 1973 several experts predicted a giant earthquake would level San Francisco, California. The day and hour the earthquake was to occur were accurately known. Radio and television talk show hosts spent hours in discussion and deliberation with experts in order to inform people of the event as well as to determine the believability of the prediction. On the day the earthquake was to occur business went on as normal. Even though all of the high buildings were supposed to be leveled, all activities functioned as usual. Businessmen entered their offices and carried on their normal daily activities as if in defiance of the great quake itself. The appointed hour came—no quake occurred. People continued to carry on their normal activities, perhaps a little more confident that the claims of the psychics, occultists, and even the saucerians have no relevance to reality.

Yet in the midst of all this complacency earthquakes, tidal waves, and volcanic eruptions are commonplace in our human experience. Whenever I travel to the east coast people constantly ask how I can stand to live in California with those terrible earthquakes that continually devastate our land. Yet, admittedly, I have never planned a day around an expected earthquake or worried about one taking place. In May of 1973, when speaking to a group of science teachers in Hawaii, news reached us of a large volcanic eruption on the Big Island. I was amazed that people accepted it as such a common disaster. There seemed to be no fear of the eruption but merely an in-rush of new tourists who wanted to catch sight of a live volcano spewing fire and lava around the countryside.

When we consider the devastation caused by flash floods, hurricanes, and other natural disasters such as cyclones, and tornadoes, can we really ignore the prophetic claims of destructions of momentous proportions? When we add to this the claims of the saucerians that man will bring about his own destruction through the use of atomic warefare and weapons, can we ignore their persistent message? Do we seem duty bound to accept and perhaps even worship anything that seems scientific? Is it possible that in our quest for scientific achievement and our search for knowledge to help us understand the universe that we could, as the saucerians claim, be bringing about our own destruction? After all, Doomsday has been predicted and we must realize from our past experience that whole civilizations have been destroyed by disasters. Look at the judgment of Sodom and Gomorrah, where two decadent cities were violently consumed by flaming fire. Legends of the lost continent and civilization of Atlantis should cause us to wonder if such events are literally possible. What of the volcanic eruptions of Pompeii and Popocatepetl? Are we to ignore these past destructions like an ostrich, telling ourselves they never occurred? Consider also the claims of psychics who predict that whole islands like Puerto Rico will sink into a boiling sea within seventeen minutes after a giant volcanic eruption. New land masses and volcanic islands will be formed off the southeast coast of the United States. The rise and fall of islands in the sea will create giant tidal waves that will sweep the Florida coast as billions of gallons of sea water inundate the entire state with water. The wave of this destruction will cause the sinking of Florida into the sea. The disasters will continue as billions and billions of gallons of water flow northward, swamping Georgia, the Carolinas, Virginia, Washington, D.C., Philadelphia, Baltimore, and finally New York City. In similar fashion Alaska, California, and Hawaii will be destroyed by giant earthquakes. The islands of Japan will disappear into a bottomless sea. The same type of destruction is predicted for the coast of Europe, as England also will sink below the waves.

As if this is not enough there will be periods of drought and famine. Dams and dikes will break, again creating havoc among the inhabitants of the land. In many instances specific messages of destruction have been given to psychics and to contactees from these beings from outer space. Many of these disasters will be caused by our continued interest in nuclear energy which, if not stopped, will cause a holocaust that will destroy our world. There will be plagues of unnerving proportions; whole populations will be wiped out. It is predicted that the earth will tilt on its axis, the polarized ice caps will melt and violent upheavals in the polar regions will play a dramatic part in these tremendous disasters.

Careful examination of the claims reveal that every major area of the earth will be struck by some type of natural disaster. It is predicted that these will take place in a thirty-to-forty-year period and that we are in this period now. These destructions will take their toll by the year 2000. In addition, it is claimed that objects from space will come crashing to earth.

In the midst of these claims of impending doom and disaster loom the visits of the saucerians and their offers of help. But how is their help possible? Ancient records reveal much of the same claims concerning the destruction of the planet Earth.

Some theologians and scholars call this a time of testing or judgment. It is even claimed by Biblical scholars that these predictions of Doomsday and devastation are not new. The modern-day prophet of doom is simply giving explicit predictions of that which was prophesied thousands of years ago in the Biblical record. In order to fully understand this phenomenon let us examine the evidence and consider the warnings of the saucerians and their insistent claim that they have come to prepare man for these judgments, as well as the fascinating proposition that those who believe will be taken off this planet to escape the impending doom. Let us turn our attention to the Bible to see if such predictions and conclusions are plausible.

Oh-Ho instructed his Canadian contactee to read the book of Revelation. It would seem logical that this would be a good place to start. The book of Revelation was written by the apostle John and is basically a prophecy of the end times. Chapters 6 through 19 describe a period of time which Biblical scholars call the "Great Tribulation." The opening verse of Chapter 6 describes the Lamb, which in the context is the Lord Jesus Christ, who is opening a seven sealed book. At the opening of each of the seals a particular judgment or event occurs on the planet Earth. It is during the opening of the first four seals that the famous Four Horsemen of the Apocalypse appear. These judgments refer to a period of peace, then war, famine, and ultimately death. According to the prophecies one-fourth of the earth's population will die through war and famine. As the sixth seal is opened we read in Revelation 6: 12–17:

. . . Lo, there was a great earthquake; and the sun became black as sackcloth of hair, and the moon became as blood;

And the stars of heaven fell unto the earth, even as a fig tree casteth her untimely figs, when she is shaken of a mighty wind.

And the heaven departed as a scroll when it is rolled together; and every mountain and island were moved out of their places.

And the kings of the earth, and the great men, and the rich men, and the chief captains, and the mighty men, and every bondman, and every free man, hid themselves in the dens and in the rocks of the mountains;

And said to the mountains and rocks, Fall on us, and hide us from the face of him that sitteth on the throne, and from the wrath of the Lamb:

For the great day of his wrath is come; and who shall be able to stand?

Here is a warning recorded by the apostle John almost nineteen hundred years ago that tells of similar destructions and which give credence to Oh-Ho's claims. In Chapter 8, verse 5, we are told that an angel took a heavenly censer, filled it with fire from the heavenly altar, and cast it to the earth; there were voices, thunderings, lightnings, and an earthquake. This event, which took place at the opening of the seventh seal, revealed another series of judgments on the earth.

In the thirteenth verse of Chapter 11 we are told of another great earthquake wherein one-tenth of a city falls and in the earthquake seven thousand men lose their lives. Those that remain will recognize that this event, where two prophets were carried off into heaven and a destructive earthquake followed, came from the hand of a powerful God. In Chapter 16 we are given insight into a final set of judgments. In verses 18 and 19a John tells us, "there were voices, and thunders, and lightnings; and there was a great earthquake, such as was not since men were upon the earth, so mighty an earthquake and so great. And the city was divided into three parts, and the cities of the nations fell. . . ."

Verses 20 and 21 continue, "And every island fled away, and the mountains were not found. And there fell upon men a great hail out of heaven, every stone about the weight of a talent: and men blasphemed God because of the plague of the Hail; for the plague thereof was exceeding great." The prophetic events pictured in the book of Revelation would certainly give us insight into the reality of the great cataclysms to come.

But such prophecies are not limited to the book of Revelation. An apostle named Peter, who also walked with Christ, predicted similar events and even went so far as to tell us the description of the heavens and the earth during the day of the Lord (a phrase used by Biblical writers to describe this period of tribulation). In the second book of Peter, Chapter 3, verse 10, we are told that this event will come quickly and catch people unawares as a thief that comes in the night. When this day comes we are told that:

The heavens shall pass away with a great noise, and the elements shall melt with fervent heat, the earth also and the works that are therein shall be burned up.

Seeing then that all these things shall be dissolved, what manner of persons ought ye to be in all holy conversation and godliness?

Looking for and hasting unto the coming of the day of God, wherein the heavens being on fire shall be dissolved, and the elements shall melt with fervent heat?

Nevertheless we, according to his promise, look for new heavens and a new earth, wherein dwelleth righteousness.

—verses 10–13

It is interesting to note that he is promising believers in

Christ that after this destruction there will be a new heaven and a new earth. Again the same promise that Oh-Ho spoke of was recorded by Peter some nineteen hundred years ago.

The apostle Paul in his first letter to the Thessalonians, Chapter 4, verses, 4–18, talks to believers of Jesus Christ and states:

> For if we believe that Jesus died and rose again, even so them also which sleep in Jesus will God bring with him.

> For this we say unto you by the word of the Lord, that we which are alive and remain unto the coming of the Lord shall not prevent them which are asleep.

> For the Lord himself shall descend from heaven with a shout, with the voice of the archangel, and with the trump of God: and the dead in Christ shall rise first:

> Then we which are alive and remain shall be caught up together with them in the clouds, to meet the Lord in the air: and so shall we ever be with the Lord.

> Wherefore comfort one another with these words.

Here he predicts that Christ will return for His followers, that they will be taken out of this world, meeting Him in the air.

But when will this event take place? Many Biblical scholars feel the answer to this question is found in the book of Revelation. In Chapter 3, verse 7, John describes the true church of brotherly love, the church of Philadelphia. These people have kept the word of God and have not denied the name of Christ. They have heeded the warnings of the Bible and, because of their faithfulness, are promised in verse 10 that they will be kept from the hour of temptation that will come to the earth. Applying this position to the true believer it is felt they will be kept from the Great Tribulation. Paul says that Christ will return for His own, meeting them in the air. Considering that in the light of what we have just read in the book of Revelation, this event, which is known as the "rapture," will take place before these great cataclysms. Again note the similarities to the claims of Oh-Ho that Christ will return, that He will take His true believers with Him out of this earth, and that the earth will go through a period of tribulation.

Considering that the saucerians claim to be preparing for the return of Jesus Christ, let us examine His testimony as recorded in the book of Matthew, Chapter 24. As Christ's disciples gathered around Him on the Mount of Olives they asked a question in verse 3 concerning the end time. They asked for a sign of His coming and of the end of the world. Jesus answered them in verses 4–13:

... Take heed that no man deceive you.

For many shall come in my name, saying, I am Christ; and shall deceive many.

And ye shall hear of wars and rumours of wars: see that ye be not troubled: for all these things must come to pass, but the end is not yet.

For nation shall rise against nation, and kingdom against kingdom: and there shall be famines, and pestilences, and earthquakes, in divers places.

All these are the beginning of sorrows.

Then shall they deliver you up to be afflicted, and shall kill you: and ye shall be hated of all nations for my name's sake.

And then shall many be offended, and shall betray one another, and shall hate one another.

And many false prophets shall rise, and shall deceive many.

And because iniquity shall abound, the love of many shall wax cold.

But he that shall endure unto the end, the same shall be saved.

He continues with a description of the Great Tribulation in verses 21–23 and warns of false Christs in verses 24–26.

For there shall arise false Christs, and false prophets, and shall shew great signs and wonders; insomuch that, if it were possible, they shall deceive the very elect.

Behold, I have told you before.

Wherefore if they shall say unto you, Behold, He is in the desert; go not forth: behold, he is in the secret chambers; believe it not.

He warns of the truth of these words in verses 35 and 36.

Heaven and earth shall pass away, but my words shall not pass away.

But of that day and hour knoweth no man, no, not the angels of heaven, but my Father only.

He describes His coming and the impending disasters and judgments as similar to the days of Noah before the destruction of the great Flood (verses 37–42).

But as the days of Noe were, so shall also the coming
of the Son of man be.

For as in the days that were before the flood they were
eating and drinking, marrying and giving in marriage,
until the day that Noe entered into the ark,

And knew not until the flood came, and took them all
away; so shall also the coming of the Son of man be.

Then shall two be in the field; the one shall be taken,
and the other left.

Two women shall be grinding at the mill; the one shall
be taken, and the other left.

Watch therefore: for ye know not what hour your
Lord doth come.

In this passage, which tells of the prophetic future of
Christ's return with great cataclysms and judgments
and ultimately the setting up of His kingdom upon this
earth, we find a strong similarity to the predictions of
the saucerians who tell of impending disasters and warn
of the return of Christ and say they are here to proclaim His kingdom. Considering the strong similarities
of their messages, the vivid prophecies of the Bible,
and the statements that Christ will return, are we to
conclude that the saucerians are here to fulfill the Biblical record? Or is there another meaning to the striking
similarities in their claims and the statements of the
Bible? When we consider the strong Biblical warning
against accepting any other message, even from an angel
from heaven, should we give any serious consideration
to their message at all? Perhaps the key to understanding their predictions lies in the meaning placed
upon them by advocates of UFOlogy. Then, and only

then, can we fully understand the implications of this new religion.

What is their motive and what is the meaning of their message? Before we can reach any valid conclusion and fully predict the effect of their return it becomes necessary to examine closely their claims and the meaning placed upon them by advocates of UFOlogy. Then and only then can we fully understand the relevance to the Biblical record and predict with accuracy the results of their return.

FIVE

The Meaning

Advocates of UFOlogy are so varied in their interests in the subject matter that it is often difficult to obtain a clear understanding of the meaning of the visits of the saucerians. Literally hundreds of books have been written on the subject of extraterrestrial visitation. They present us with a vast number of viewpoints concerning the saucerians themselves. It is interesting that although there are numerous claims covering a wide number of fields—from the origin of man on this earth to ancient civilizations, technological warnings, prophetic fulfillment of Biblical prophecy, which includes complete religious significance as these visitors are proclaimed to be gods—there is little disagreement or argument among advocates of UFOlogy. In most cases the concept (regardless of which concept is chosen) is presented as a possible explanation in an attempt to ascertain the meaning of these visits from space. Since it is the purpose of this book to identify the saucerians and to predict the outcome of these visitations, we will try in this chapter to survey the various claims in an attempt to gain the true meaning of these visitations.

A popular concept is that UFOs are chariots of the gods. It is felt by advocates of this position that highly advanced beings from outside our solar system visited this planet in the past and are responsible for the creation of humans here. The premise goes something like this: considering that we are very advanced in our technology and have gained the ability to travel to other planets in our solar system, it is likely that there are beings living on other planets in other solar systems who have also achieved the same degree of technology and although we have never observed another planet outside our solar system and have no scientific, empirical evidence that they exist, it is assumed that there are many of these highly developed civilizations throughout our universe. And, since we are postulating travel at the speed of light, it is possible that some of these highly advanced creatures on one of these proposed planets outside our galaxy have already developed the ability to travel at the speed of light, thus making visitation to our planet possible.

Because of the inability of scientists to demonstrate the evolutionary development of man upon this planet and because of the distinct differences between man and the ape, signified by the fact that man has the capacity to speak and to build and to invent by use of his highly developed brain, it is suggested that these highly advanced visitors from outer space played a part in the development of man upon this planet. Reportedly the earth was visited some forty thousand years ago and certain apes were selected for experimentation. By the use of genetic engineering these intelligent visitors took the first step in creating man upon this earth. This is based on the assumption that man today is highly intelligent and is learning something about his own genetic structure.

It is predicted that in the near future, because of our new advanced techniques, a woman will be able to go to the supermarket and purchase a sperm cell of her choice. The label on the package in the freezer will accurately predict the hair color, eye color, skin color, approximate height, intelligence, and sex of the individual who will be born. The woman can then take her package to the local doctor and by artificial insemination plan the birth of the child for whenever convenient. Since we are contemplating such activities, obviously highly intelligent creatures who have the ability to travel at the speed of light must have already conceived of this type of genetic manipulation. Taking some cells and implanting them artificially in the female apes that had been carefully selected, creatures more similar to man came into existence. Allowing these half-man/half-ape mutants to evolve for another thirty thousand years or so, these saucerians reportedly returned to earth seven thousand years ago. Taking specimens of these newly developed creatures with them, they, again by artificial insemination, produced the perfect race of man.

Although there is no basis of fact for such speculation, it is felt by advocates of this position that such manipulation of ape-like creatures to produce humans is consistent with what is found in the Bible. The gods in reality created humans from these ape-like creatures. The Bible speaks of woman being created from the rib of a man and, considering that our modern technology has demonstrated that every cell in the body carries the template and the genetic code for the whole body, it is felt that this supports the creation of man and woman by genetic manipulation.

The fall of man as described in the Bible, where man disobeyed and fell into sin, is described by UFO advocates as the disobedience of these newly formed perfect beings who have sexual relations with the half-man/half-ape creatures, thus creating a fallen, inferior race of which we are all descendants. This leaves us with two races—the sons of man (fallen creatures) and the sons of god (created by the saucerians). Although such an explanation is given in an attempt to fulfill the Biblical statement of the creation of Adam and Eve, it fails to indicate where the other animals come from, how the ape originated on this earth, and therefore ignores the Biblical premise that all things were created by God in the beginning. The Bible presents the picture that all things, including the physical universe itself, were created by the power of a supernatural God.

Although this position attempts to explain the creation of man and woman by superintelligent beings because of the failure of evolution to explain the development of man, it fails to answer the question of where life came from in the beginning. If man on this planet is the result of genetic manipulation by supertechnological beings from outer space and we accept this conclusion in order to explain the origin of intelligent man, because evolution has failed to do so, then how do we explain the development of highly intelligent supertechnological beings on other planets? If it is impossible for man to have evolved by chance on earth, would it not be equally impossible for supertechnological beings to have evolved by chance on other planets? If genetic manipulation is necessary for the development of man on this planet and we must seek extraterrestrial visitors to explain the origin of man, how do we explain the origin of these extraterrestrial visitors? Who is responsible for them? What is the force or power or being that artificially inseminated creatures on their own planets to produce these intelligent saucerians? The concept of extraterrestrial visitors used as an explanation for the development of intelligent life on this earth has a serious defect in its logic and only begs the question concerning the origin of man without ever answering this problem or, for that matter, even raising the question.

It is proposed (by this theory) that these extraterrestrial visitors continued to visit our planet and were worshipped and accepted as gods throughout recorded history. It is claimed that the building of the great pyramids in Egypt, Mexico, and South America were influenced by these saucerians, and that structures such as obelisks and giant statues found in many ancient civilizations were constructed under the supervision of extraterrestrial visitors. The concept that man has worshipped gods from outer space who have a high degree of technology is supposedly represented in many cave drawings and artifacts which seem to depict spacemen. Supposedly man was primitive and could not accomplish these feats without outside help from these beings. This is based on the assumption that we are highly intelligent and yet we cannot understand how these various feats, such as the moving of thousands of huge stones from quarries to make pyramids, were accomplished. Even with our high degree of technology such undertakings would be hard to explain. Again the Bible is used to support such a conclusion, as it talks of strange visitors from the skies such as the fiery chariot that came to pick up the prophet Elijah and the strange vision of four living creatures and a wheel within a wheel described by Ezekiel. It would be very difficult to accept that these are visitations of saucerians to Ezekiel and Elijah if we did not already have a preconceived idea of space visitation. These could very well be fiery chariots and the visitation of four strange living beasts sent directly by God with a distinct message for Ezekiel.

Since proponents of UFOlogy attempt to accept the Bible literally we bring up this interesting question in our discussion: Are we to accept the Bible as a basis of all truth and evaluate all theories in light of the Bible, or are we to reinterpret the Bible to fit into our pet theories? As already noted in the comments concerning the creation of man by genetic manipulation, only a part of the Biblical record was used and it was used to support the theory. If, on the other hand, one would accept the Biblical record and realize that the God of the Bible created two perfect individuals, Adam and Eve, who disobeyed God because they were deceived by Satan, a fallen angel, therefore resulting in a fallen race, we would realize that the fall involves separation from God and an edict that all men born into this world would die. The beings created were still perfect in regards to intelligence. We are told immediately that in the period that followed their children began to build cities. Keep in mind also that a hut or a village is not a city. The cities described in the Bible, such as Babylon and Nineveh, have all proved to be marvels for archaeologists. In addition, Genesis 4 describes the descendants of Cain, the first son born of Adam and Eve. Not only did he build a city and name it after his son, but we are told that his descendants raised cattle and played musical instruments such as the harp and organ. One of his descendants, Tubalcain, was competent in the use of brass and iron. Surely people with the intelligence to build cities, domesticate animals, raise food, and use brass and iron are far different from primitive nomads. Such a concept is drastically different from the concept of gradual development of these skills over a long period of time, as proposed by those who hold to the theory of evolution. Such a concept is far different from the concept that man acquired these abilities from proposed extraterrestrial visitors from some speculated planet in an unknown galaxy. Since the current message of the saucerians predicts a fulfillment of the Bible that seems consistent with the text, why do these areas concerning the beginning upon which these future prophecies are based differ drastically from the Biblical record? Perhaps the answer to this question can only be determined by a further look at the religious claims of these new advocates of UFOlogy.

Jesus Christ was a saucerian. That is the claim of many followers of the new religion of UFOlogy. He came to this earth to guide and lead people into a new direction. After His death and resurrection He ascended into a cloud or saucer and was carried away into the heavens. Is such an explanation possible?

Many advocates of UFOlogy find this belief basic to an understanding of the Bible and, with messiah-like fervor, they proclaim the message in an attempt to convince mankind of the reality of His return. The entire Bible is thus reinterpreted from its traditional framework in order to fit into the new religion of UFOlogy. Without really explaining the problems involved in the beginning or even attempting to explain the origin of the heavens and the earth, the Bible is placed into a new context and framework which is basically that of saucer visitation.

If we assume the premise that people have been visited by beings from outer space then whole areas of the Bible must be reinterpreted. This then is the basic meaning of the modern interest in flying saucers and the religion advocated by UFOlogy.

The sons of God mentioned in Genesis 6 are believed to be spacemen who were for some reason visiting our planet. Whatever the reason, they had sexual relations with the daughters of man. There is some similarity here concerning the concept mentioned before concerning the sons of God and the sons of man. But there is a serious discrepancy as to who the sons of God really are. In one explanation they are the perfect men created in the beginning, taken by the saucerians to live with them and on occasion sent back to us—Christ, Buddha, Confucius, and other great leaders who imparted knowledge to our world. In other accounts the sons of God are not remnants of created men but the saucerians themselves. Both of these views differ from the traditional view the church has held for many centuries, that the sons of God were angels and the daughters of man were simply the fallen female descendants of the first pair God created on this earth.

The key to one's interpretation of Scripture seems to rest on the identity of the sons of God. Accepting either of the first two views requires a drastic change in Scripture itself, thereby forcing us to reinterpret many events in the light of saucer visitations. The traditional view does not require any special interpretation of the Bible but fits well within the established framework of Biblical interpretation.

If flying saucers were visiting our planet there would have been no necessity for Noah to build an ark to escape the great Flood. He could simply have escaped in a flying saucer as the gods would certainly warn him of such an impending disaster. Since the Bible records the building of the ark and the gathering of animals one might ask why such an event was necessary. Although this deviates from what the Bible states it is felt by UFOlogists that for some unknown reason the saucerians wanted samples of all the animals living on the earth and so a saucerian posing as God instructed Noah to build an ark and gather all the animals in one place so they could have two of every kind. Although they do not tell us what happened to Noah or if it is as the Bible states, it is believed that Noah, his family, the ark, and its cargo were transported by a saucer to some other planet. Whether this was to be a type of celestial zoo or a complete set of research animals and guinea pigs for the saucerians on their home planet or a cargo of species of animals and men especially gathered to fill a Garden of Eden on some new planet is purely left to our imaginations. The concept of the Flood and the total devastation as told in the Bible is completely ignored. If the Biblical record is to have any authority it seems strange that man, in an attempt to use the Bible as his source of authority, picks and chooses what he considers truth.

Continuing in this same vein, it is theorized that Moses was contacted by saucerians because the Bible reports he communicated with God. In secret meetings he was instructed on the building of the Ark of the Covenant which many UFOlogists feel was a type of radio receiver and transmitter. Here Moses received his instructions from the saucerians who traveled ahead of Israel in a luminous object shaped like a cloud. Although there is absolutely no evidence that the Ark of the Covenant built by Moses was a transmitter, and electronic experts have indicated that such a concept is impossible, this again is another claim of these new advocates of UFOlogy.

Reportedly saucerians guided the Israelites out of

Egypt, taking them out of the bondage of Pharaoh, using some means of antigravity to part the waters of the Red Sea, guiding these people to the land of Palestine. What is hard to understand in such a concept is the fact that other proponents of flying saucer visitation claim that the great civilizations of Egypt with their pyramids and obelisks and great statues were built with the help of extraterrestrial visitors. It was necessary for the Egyptians to have slaves in order to build these great structures for their highly intelligent gods. Is it logical to also expect these visitors to destroy the system they had made by sending a man named Moses to bring plagues upon their Egyptian followers? That they would literally destroy the economy of Egypt and would bring death upon the first-born child simply to free some slaves? It does not seem likely that one would go to the trouble to build a great and mighty civilization to gain the worship and admiration of the Egyptians only to destroy them later.

The message of the book of Exodus is very clear— the God of Moses and the Israelites is a great and more powerful God than the Egyptians' god. In each of the confrontations between Moses and Pharaoh the very point of the message was that the God of the Bible, the God of Moses, was the true God. The concept that Moses was visited by extraterrestrial beings leaves much to be desired and many unanswered questions. If we accept the concept that there are opposing gods and opposing beings from different parts of the galaxy who are vying for the worship and fellowship of man, the question again arises concerning their intelligence, their technology, and their origin. It remains a major mystery. Who are we to believe?

There are several other instances in the Bible which must be reinterpreted. Take, for instance, the story of Lot in the cities of Sodom and Gomorrah, as told in Genesis 19: 1–28. Lot was warned by angels that the cities of Sodom and Gomorrah would be destroyed. The men of the town came to Lot and asked that he send out the angels that they might have sexual relations with them. As a result the men of the city were struck blind. Lot then was told to flee the city and, according to advocates of UFOlogy, some atomic explosive device had already been triggered and he must escape this nuclear explosion. Lot fled the city.

The use of an atomic explosion seems strange in the light of the message today where men are warned constantly to lay aside nuclear weapons, to stop our experiments with atomic energy because the saucerians have long ago learned that this is the wrong type of power. Yet if they have been visiting our planet for a number of years and are truly what they are believed to be, does it not seem inconsistent that we are told on the one hand that the saucerians leveled the cities of Sodom and Gomorrah by atomic explosion and on the other that we should have nothing to do with atomic power?

If an atomic destruction took place, where is the evidence? In the area of Sodom and Gomorrah there are great deposits of salt, sulfur, and bitumen as well as an abundance of natural gas and oil deposits in what is known as the Great Rift Valley. Another startling possibility explains this destruction. Considering that the Dead Sea is thirteen hundred feet below the level of the Mediterranean Sea and that the northern part of the Dead Sea is thirteen hundred feet deeper still and that there are great faults in this area it seems more logical that the destruction of Sodom and Gomorrah was caused by a great earthquake. God, who warned of this destruction by sending His angels to warn Lot and his family, caused the earth to quake thereby disturbing the natural gas which ignited with the salt, sulfur, and bitumen to cause complete destruction of these cities. There is good geological evidence that such an eruption took place, since great quantities of the earth's surface are clearly visible high on the mountainside of Mount Sodom. Remember, this possibility is further emphasized by the fact that the word "brimstone" used in the Biblical story means bituminous material and this certainly seems to be a more logical explanation.

Why then do advocates of UFOlogy insist on making claims that require reinterpretations of the Bible? Basically the purpose of this reinterpretation is to explain away the miraculous element in the Bible. For man has difficulty accepting that which he cannot understand and so, in an attempt to explain the miracles of the Bible without reliance upon a supernatural God, advocates of UFOlogy have proposed saucer intervention and advanced technology. One proponent of this concept honestly states his whole purpose in adopting this new viewpoint is to explain away the miracles of the Bible; he proposes that God is not supernatural but supertechnological. Although we cannot comprehend or understand the technology of the saucerians we can put our faith in a technology that is higher or more advanced than ours. The basic reason for the conclusion that technology should replace miracles lies in the claim that every effect must have a cause and therefore all things must be explainable by some natural means. Reliance upon miracles is like having an effect without a cause. Yet this same individual is very inconsistent for he tells us that man was created by saucerians and neglects to say where these saucerians had their beginning. He would believe and maintain that all animals and plants on this planet are the result of a chance process of evolution with no purpose or reason for their existence, that life itself came from nonliving material, that that which has none of the capacities or properties of life, dead matter, is responsible for life itself. That man with his capacity of speech and his ability to think is ultimately the result of particles of matter that randomly, through some process we cannot understand, became living material. Is this in reality consistent with the concept of cause and effect?

Can we believe that man and/or saucerians are the result of dead matter? And what about the universe, the planets, stars, galaxies, the complexity of the universe itself—where did it come from, where is it going? Here again is an effect without a cause. How does one explain the existence of planets revolving around the sun, the moons revolving around their planets, and the literally billions of stars. Are they eternal? No one really believes they are. It is claimed they had a beginning but again what was the cause? Postulating that the God of the Bible is merely an extraterrestrial visitor does not solve the origin of man or the origin of the planet Earth. It does not solve the problem of miracles. It does not explain the mystery of life. It simply begs the question. To use the argument of cause and effect is not valid when we attempt to explain the origin of the universe, life, and man. The argument of cause and effect would demand some power or force to organize all things in the beginning. That power or force must be a supernatural God, not a supertechnological one. In our attempt to understand the meaning of life itself let us not be so willing to throw away Biblical truth because of our fear of the unexplainable or of miracles but let us instead use that truth as an empirical standard in order to gain insight into the reality and meaning of life.

Considering the failure of this premise to explain the ultimate cause and origin of a saucerian god or gods, is it necessary to change one's belief in miracles? For again, in an attempt to make the Bible relevant to the new saucerian technology the attempt is made to explain away even the miracles of Christ. For Christ reportedly was a saucerian and all miraculous events associated with His life are explained with saucer technology. The Bible states that Christ was born of a virgin named Mary. Rather than deny it, it is proposed that the angel Gabriel used some type of hypnotic device on Mary, and that while she was in a hypnotic trance artificial insemination was performed using the sperm of God, who in this case was the leader of the saucerians. They used some type of hypodermic needle and Mary retained her virginity. She in reality believed that the seed was that of the Holy Spirit and was unaware that she was in the power of beings from outer space. The star of Bethlehem was nothing more than a hovering, luminous, flying saucer, which explains how it could lead wise men and shepherds to a particular house and thus to some extent give the appearance of a miracle.

It is claimed that since little is known of the life of Jesus that God did not tell all to the writers of Scripture. Obviously He does not lie to them but He does hold things back, not revealing all of the truth. It is believed then that during the early life of Christ He was instructed by the saucerians and indoctrinated and may have even practiced the use of His powers in order that His miracles would seem believable. He may, we are told, have had to undergo some biological changes. During the thirty-year period before He began His earthly ministry the saucerians were busy gathering people to set the stage for the drama to come. By hypnotizing them they became blind, had withered hands, or became lame and thus were prepared for the healing miracles of Christ. As Christ entered a city and met a blind man He could tell him that his sight was restored and of course the blind man saw because he had been programmed to accept the post-hypnotic suggestion of the being known as Jesus. Thus UFOlogists explain away the healing miracles of Christ, all by post-hypnotic suggestion controlled, naturally, by the saucerians. The only position is that Jesus actually had supernatural power to heal the sick. Obviously, we are told such a conclusion is unwarranted because Christ never restored a missing limb to anybody. If He really possessed the power to heal the sick, the lame, and the blind, why did He not heal everyone? Why did He pick only certain cases to heal? Obviously the saucerians were busy bringing to Jesus only the beings that had been programmed to accept His post-hypnotic suggestions. Others, by use of similar hypnotic suggestions, were kept from coming in contact with the being Jesus.

It is also believed that neither Jesus nor anyone else can perform an act in defiance of natural law, that in reality He only brought hypnotized subjects out of a trance. This conclusion is necessary because He never restored people's missing limbs. It is interesting to note, however, that the Bible does record the fact that Peter cut off the ear of one of the soldiers who came to arrest Christ before the crucifixion and that Christ picked up the ear and replaced it. This certainly is a miraculous event and cannot be explained by hypnotic trance. It would seem that the restoring of an ear is equally as miraculous as restoring a limb. That occurrence places serious doubt on the statements of UFOlogists that Christ was not able to perform miracles.

What of the miracle of Cana, where by a simple verbal command Christ changed the relatively simple molecular structure of water into the more highly complex structure of wine? This is a pure reversal of the Second Law of Thermodynamics which states that the natural order of things is to go from the complex to the simple. Surely this demonstrates an ability and power over natural law that defies our explanation unless we accept the premise that Christ was supernatural.

In order to explain the raising of Lazarus from the dead with the help of saucerians, we must believe that highly intelligent people who were accustomed to burying their dead failed to realize that Lazarus was simply in a hypnotic trance. The same is to be said of the ruler's daughter in Matthew 9. Upon hearing Jesus' comment that she was asleep, not dead, the people laughed and yet He touched her hand and she arose. The reaction of the people indicates that they were aware of what death was. In the case of Lazarus, who was already in the grave, the body was already decaying, as is known by the fact that witnesses reported "he stinketh." Again Christ called to Lazarus and he rose from the dead which signifies a miraculous power was involved. Since the saucerians claim no power over death and express a fear of death themselves it is obvious that they cannot bring one back from the grave. It is hard to imagine that in the province of Palestine, under the control of the Roman government, they were so primitive that they could not recognize when a person was dead.

Again the supernatural content of the Bible is attacked on the basis that Christ, during His earthly ministry, cast out demons. One major criticism of this practice states that if Jesus possessed supernatural powers He would have realized there is no such thing as demon possession. What is the basis for such a conclusion? If man is a created being who fell because of temptation by Satan, and if Satan and his followers are in control of man to the extent that it was necessary for God to send His Son to free man from the bondage of sin, it would seem a logical conclusion that men are so engulfed by their defiance of God's law as to be literally possessed. There are so many modern cases of demon possession and the exorcising of demons that one merely needs to read the daily newspaper to verify their existence. To maintain that there are neither demons nor demonic possession, but that Jesus knew these people's brains were malfunctioning because of a brain-wave manipulator and used post-hypnotic suggestion to return the individual's brain to normal seems ludicrous. Are we really to believe that saucerians have gone to this much trouble to perpetrate a fraud on the inhabitants of the earth? Was it necessary to attempt this type of mass hypnosis in order to gain the worship of man?

Considering that the Romans already had a highly developed system of worship of gods and that they obtained their concept of those gods from the civilizations of the past, who reportedly had already been visited and were under the control of these saucerians, why was it necessary to change the mode of operation at this time, proposing a new god to replace the old ones? There is no reason for such a position unless we accept the Bible as literal and accept the concept that the God who created man and brought His people out of bondage in Egypt was once again offering to people the opportunity to return to fellowship and worship by cleansing their sins through His Son, Jesus Christ. It is always the belief in other gods, whether they be Roman, Greek, Babylonian, or Egyptian, that creates the necessity for judgment, repentance, and a return to the one true God of the Bible. All of history revolves around this point. All of the Bible was written to reveal the one true God. Can there really be any truth to the claim that this true God is merely the head of a group of extraterrestrial visitors upon our planet? There certainly seems no reason to attempt to explain away the miracles of the Bible and the miracles of Christ simply because they are outside natural law. Certainly the God who created the heavens and the earth, the God who created man, the God who created life has the ability and power to control, change, and manipulate the natural laws He established. It seems more reasonable to accept this premise than the concept that saucerians who simply evolved from unknown creatures on unknown areas of the universe have controlled the life and destiny of those on the planet Earth.

When we realize the foolishness of the claims that the saucerians perpetrated a fraud upon the people living in the time of Christ in an attempt to mislead the people of that day into believing in miracles, when the saucerians knew that we, with our superintelligence, would be able to discover the explanation of saucer technology. Why not instead reveal themselves in power, demonstrating who they are? Why attempt to fool people through the use of so-called miracles?

In the feeding of the five thousand it is claimed that Jesus, son of the head saucerian, made the people lie on the ground with their faces hidden so they would not see the food being lowered from the saucer above. The people were to lie in groups of fifty or one hundred so the saucerians could easily count them from their saucer high above the earth and know how much food to lower. But surely, out of five thousand someone would look, someone would peek, someone would notice the food coming down from heaven and reveal the miracle as a hoax. Surely, with all of Christ's enemies who wanted Him silenced because of His teachings, a witness could have been produced to tell of this strange phenomenon of food being lowered from the saucer. If the saucerians wanted to deceive the people and if the people were so uneducated as to believe that Christ ascended into the clouds when actually He left in a saucer, would they not have believed in another miracle if they just sat on the ground and watched the food come down from clouds? Would this not also have sufficed as a miraculous event? There seems no need to have hidden their faces. An accurate reading of the feeding of the five thousand, as found in Mark 6, verses 37–44, indicates that the people only sat down upon the green grass. Although they sat in ranks by hundreds and fifties, there is no indication that they were asked to hide their faces. Instead they were allowed to look at Christ who took two fishes and five loaves and broke them up, blessed them, and gave them to His disciples. This food fed all of the five thousand people and there were twelve baskets of food left over. Certainly this was an unexplainable event unless we accept that Christ had the power to perform miracles.

It is interesting that proponents of UFOlogy even attempt to explain away the crucifixion and resurrection of Jesus Christ. It is stated that this being, Jesus, obviously could not be supernatural because among the three men crucified He was the first to die. If He truly possessed supernatural strength, would He not have lasted long after the two mortals had died? We are told that when the soldiers came to examine Him three hours after the crucifixion one of them, under the direction of the saucerians (through mind manipulation or hypnosis), cast his spear into Jesus' side, thereby piercing His flesh to fulfill an ancient prophecy. Certainly no other conclusion is necessary unless we believe God took hold of the soldier and forced him to move his hand. It is never mentioned that a supernatural God who had the power to create all things in the beginning and who knows totally all future events and has prophesied them would have known what the soldier would do, thus making it very easy to foretell the event long before it occurred. Yet, because of a refusal to accept a supernatural God, we are told that the suffering of Jesus on the cross was controlled through hypnosis by beings aboard their saucer.

This saucer had been manipulated to come in direct alignment with the sun, and cause the appearance of darkness. When Jesus cried out on the cross, "Why have you forsaken Me?" it was because the pain He was bearing was greater than He had been led to believe He would have to bear. The saucerians were thrilled with this statement because it indicated that the event looked real and that Jesus was really suffering and this, of course, would make it more believable to those who were watching.

In reality, proponents of this view claim, Christ did not die on the cross. Since we realize that under hypnosis bleeding can be stopped, obviously these superintelligent saucerians also had the ability to induce bleeding, thereby giving the appearance of death. Thus Jesus, entering a hypnotic trance, was buried by His followers. In the tomb the saucerians healed His wounds, revived Him from His trance, rolled away the stone by using their saucer, and made it appear that He rose from the dead and appeared to His disciples.

Certainly if such an explanation is possible a member of the Roman guard in charge of the tomb would have noticed some saucer activity. Surely there would be some record of a hovering light or lights connected with the moving of the stone. The basis for this theory is that if Jesus Christ were a supernatural being, He would not have cried out that He was forsaken on the cross. However, when we understand that during the suffering of Jesus on the cross He carried with Him the sins of all mankind it is not surprising. Although He had great power at His disposal He chose instead this burden: that man by His death and ultimate resurrection would have a remedy for his sin. By belief in the death and resurrection of Jesus Christ man is forgiven of his sins and promised eternal life. It is the weight of mankind's sin that caused Christ's agony and suffering on the cross. It is for this reason that God turned His back on His Son, why Christ faced death alone. But He chose to face it on our behalf that we might once again have fellowship with our heavenly Father by believing in Jesus Christ. The fact that the sun was darkened only emphasizes the supernatural power of a Creator who controls all entities. The sun, moon, and stars were in His full control. This is further emphasized by the prophetic statements given in the book of Revelation concerning the sun, moon, and stars and the ultimate destruction of the heavens and the earth. The resurrection of Jesus Christ from the dead acts as a sign to us that He has the power to do what He claimed. Since He rose from the dead and triumphed over the grave, those who believe in Him are also promised life in heaven with Him.

To claim that Jesus was a product of saucerians is to deny the whole basic purpose of the Biblical record and place the concept of eternal life into a madhouse of confusion. Even so, proponents of UFOlogy claim that eternity does exist. They say that after the resurrection Jesus was carried off into heaven by a saucer, perhaps the saucer piloted by God Himself, but that He promised to-return. In an attempt to continue to fulfill the message of the Bible it is claimed that those who truly believe, who truly proclaim the message, who truly accept the concept of UFOlogy will likewise be taken into heaven to live forever.

Since there will be no sin or evil in heaven UFOlogists claim that eternity will be boring. There will be nothing to satisfy our human senses. Therefore it is proposed that our soul or the electromagnetic being which makes up our personalities and which will continue for eternity should be implanted in a plastic body where we would be able to experience the physical sensations of life. After learning about life itself and learning of the rules God has established, we will then be free to populate our own planets, to create our own worlds, to manipulate these beings the same way that God, the head saucerian, has done with the beings on this earth. To experience the physical sensations of greed, lust, and violence through the beings we have created we will become as gods to the beings we have made on our own planet.

Such a premise has absolutely no basis of fact as revealed in the Bible, nor is there any scientific reason that would indicate that such a future is possible. Such an attempt to imitate the Biblical promise of eternal life through a belief in UFOlogy and saucerians fails to understand the Biblical promise of ultimate perfection in the eternal state. Rather than be bored because of a future without bodies unable to experience physical sensations, we are promised a glorified body and a return to the perfect state that once was a heritage of humans in the Garden of Eden when Adam and Eve roamed freely on the earth. It is a state of perfection with a promise of new values, concepts, and ideas, not physical sensations or pleasures of the finite mind but the total fulfillment of that which is above man's understanding or comprehension as we abide forever in the blissful eternity prepared by an infinite God. This eternity is one where man will totally understand all of the laws and operations God has made. One where man will be perfectly in tune with his Creator, knowing and realizing for the first time the ultimate reality, presence, and perfection of the powerful Creator who loved man so much that He sent His Son to die on the cross that man might live with Him forever.

The meaning of the message of the saucerians becomes clear as we evaluate it in the light of the Biblical record. It is an attempt to substitute a natural, technological god for a supernatural God. Ultimately this message fails to provide the same promise of eternity, although it attempts to imitate that which God reveals. It falls short of the blessed promise proclaimed in the Word of God. As we understand the message of the saucerians and the meaning placed upon it by advocates of UFOlogy we wonder at the motive behind these visitations. When we consider the prophetic claims of the Bible and the duplicate messages of the saucerians themselves in their contact with beings on earth, we soon realize the dangers of this new religion. But what is the full implication of these claims? What is to be gained by this attempt at fulfillment of Biblical prophecies and the proposed reinterpretation of the Word of God?

Certainly when we realize who Jesus Christ really is, the Almighty, all-powerful Creator of the heavens and the earth as revealed by the apostle Paul in Colossians 1: 16 and 17, we see the foolishness of the claims of the saucerians and realize the impact of this great deception.

SIX

The Key

The advocates of this new religion of UFOlogy are blindly preparing people for their doom. It is true that they speak of the same disasters prophesied in the Bible and even use the Bible to support their claims. Yet they fall short of the truth of the Bible and falsify the statements concerning Christ. Why? Deliberate deception is the only possible answer to that most important question.

These so-called extraterrestrial visitors are simply parroting the message of Satan in order to deceive the inhabitants of this world and prepare for the coming of the antichrist. How? Let us examine the evidence.

Remember the statements of Oh-Ho and Ashtar? These entities claim to be visitors from outer space. Actually, as we have noted, they seem to possess their contacts and control their actions. Sound familiar? Of course it does. The Bible is full of examples of demon possession. Luke 8:26–39 records the story of a man possessed by many devils.

And they arrived at the country of the Gadarenes, which is over against Galilee.

And when he went forth to land, there met him out of the city a certain man, which had devils long time, and ware no clothes, neither abode in any house, but in the tombs.

When he saw Jesus, he cried out, and fell down before him, and with a loud voice said, What have I to do with thee, Jesus, thou Son of God most high? I beseech thee, torment me not.

(For he had commanded the unclean spirit to come out of the man. For oftentimes it had caught him: and he was kept bound with chains and in fetters; and he brake the bands, and was driven of the devil into the wilderness.)

And Jesus asked him, saying, What is thy name? And he said, Legion: because many devils were entered into him.

And they besought him that he would not command them to go out into the deep.

And there was there an herd of many swine feeding on the mountain: and they besought him that he would suffer them to enter into them.

And he suffered them.

Then went the devils out of the man, and entered into the swine: and the herd ran violently down a steep place into the lake, and were choked.

When they that fed them saw what was done, they fled, and went and told it in the city and in the country.

Then they went out to see what was done; and came to Jesus, and found the man, out of whom the devils were departed, sitting at the feet of Jesus, clothed, and in his right mind: and they were afraid.

They also which saw it told them by what means he that was possessed of the devils was healed.

Then the whole multitude of the country of the Gadarenes round about besought him to depart from them; for they were taken with great fear: and he went up into the ship, and returned back again.

Now the man out of whom the devils were departed besought him that he might be with him: but Jesus sent him away, saying,

Return to thine own house, and shew how great things God hath done unto thee. And he went his way, and published throughout the whole city how great things Jesus had done unto him.

Note that the man was completely controlled by these demons and only the power of Christ was able to free him from this horrid possession by these ungodly creatures. When we hear of such examples and read of their modern counterparts in the daily newspapers, it is not hard to visualize what is happening. Appearing as visitors from other parts of the galaxy, these entities appear unto earthlings in an attempt to lead them from the truth. Capitalizing upon our worship of technology they attempt to gain our confidence by quoting Scripture. Hoping to deceive us into accepting his message the devil is subtly leading man to a position of usefulness as he prepares for a final battle with God. Satan believes he can win if only he masses enough followers to overthrow the forces of heaven. But fortunately for believers in Christ, we already know the outcome of Satan's futile attempt. This is emphasized by the past history of people on this planet Earth.

Satan is a created entity, created perfect until iniquity was found in him. Notice the testimony of Isaiah concerning the fall of Satan (Isaiah 14:12–15):

How art thou fallen from heaven, O Lucifer, son of the morning! how art thou cut down to the ground, which didst weaken the nations!

For thou hast said in thine heart, I will ascend into heaven, I will exalt my throne above the stars of God: I will sit also upon the mount of the congregation, in the sides of the north:

I will ascend above the heights of the clouds; I will be like the most High.

Yet thou shalt be brought down to hell, to the sides of the pit.

Satan wanted to be as God. He was deceived in his heart and considered himself equal with God. Satan the anointed cherub of God fell in his own pride. Ezekiel emphasizes this in Chapter 28, verses 12–19, where he speaks of the King of Tyre, whom scholars agree is Satan.

Son of man, take up a lamentation upon the king of Tyrus, and say unto him, Thus saith the Lord God; Thou sealest up the sum, full of wisdom, and perfect in beauty.

Thou hast been in Eden the garden of God; every precious stone was thy covering, the sardius, topaz, and the diamond, the beryl, the onyx, and the hasper, the sapphire, the emerald, and the carbuncle, and gold: the workmanship of thy tabrets and of thy pipes was prepared in thee in the day that thou wast created.

Thou art the anointed cherub that covereth; and I have set thee so: thou wast upon the holy mountain of God, thou hast walked up and down in the midst of the stones of fire.

Thou wast perfect in thy ways from the day that thou wast created, till iniquity was found in thee.

By the multitude of thy merchandise they have filled the midst of thee with violence, and thou hast sinned: therefore I will cast thee as profane out of the mountain of God: and I will destroy thee, O covering cherub, from the midst of the stones of fire.

Thine heart was lifted up because of thy beauty, thou hast corrupted thy wisdom by reason of thy brightness: I will cast thee to the ground, I will lay thee before kings, that they may behold thee.

Thou hast defiled thy sanctuaries by the multitude of thine iniquities, by the iniquity of thy traffick; therefore will I bring forth a fire from the midst of thee, it shall devour thee, and I will bring thee to ashes upon the earth in the sight of all them that behold thee.

All they that know thee among the people shall be astonished at thee: thou shalt be a terror, and never shalt thou be any more.

Satan, the perfect anointed cherub of God, thought he was equal to God and rebelled. Looking upon God's creation he saw the man and woman who God had made and felt that by obtaining their worship he would somehow realize the equality he was seeking. And so he tempted man and woman with the promise that if they ate of the tree of knowledge they too would be as gods. Adam and Eve ate of the fruit and fell from the grace of God, plunging the entire human race into sin. Even though God placed a curse upon the serpent (who in reality was Satan) that promised the ultimate victory (Genesis 3:15, as a blow to the head is fatal), it is obvious that Satan still exercises control over the world in which we live. His influence is easily seen as the first child born to Adam and Eve, Cain, was a murderer. The descendants of our first parents were evil in their ways. In a little less than two thousand years the whole world was corrupt and evil permeated the land and the Word of God was almost null and void. Thus we can see the success of Satan and his followers (the one-third of the angels of heaven who revolted and fell with him) upon the early world.

But notice the description of that world. Genesis 6, verses 1–4, sheds light upon the topic of our discussion.

And it came to pass, when men began to multiply on the face of the earth, and daughters were born unto them,

That the sons of God saw the daughters of men that they were fair; and they took them wives of all which they chose.

And the Lord said, My spirit shall not always strive with man, for that he also is flesh: yet his days shall be an hundred and twenty years.

There were giants in the earth in those days: and also after that, when the sons of God came in unto the daughters of men, and they bare children to them, the same became mighty men which were of old, men of renown.

In this passage we are told that some type of extraterrestrial visitors specifically called the "sons of God" visited this planet in the not-too-distant past. Tempted by the beauty of the women living on the earth at that time, these visitors took unto themselves terrestrial wives. Evidently from the text the offspring born as a result of this uncommon union became giants in the land. This could indeed refer to physical stature or it might refer to intelligence, meaning simply that they were wiser than the normal inhabitants of the earth. Being filled with knowledge and wisdom outside of themselves we can easily understand why they became mighty men and, according to the text, were known as men of renown. Added to this concept is the possibility of extra physical stature, a combination which would indeed make such a union between the sons of God and the daughters of men desirable.

But again we are faced with a problem, for if the sons of God are indeed visitors from outer space we still have no understanding of their origin, or of the origin of the universe itself. If these sons of God are responsible for the creation of man on this earth then why is the physical union between themselves and their created creatures in need of punishment? Genesis 6:5–7 states specifically that . . .

. . . God saw the wickedness of man was great in the earth and that every imagination of the thoughts of his heart was only evil continually. And it repented the Lord that he had made man on the earth, and it grieved him at his heart. And the Lord said, I will destroy man whom I have created from the face of the earth; both man, and beast, and the creeping thing, and the fowls of the air; for it repenteth me that I have made them.

This passage indicates that there is a higher Supreme Being that is above even the sons of God and who holds them responsible for their actions. For some reason He was displeased by the attitudes and actions of man on this earth. If indeed this was a union between some extraterrestrial visitors and the descendants of man then it was greatly repulsive to God. If God is no more than the head saucerian why would such a union cause Him such displeasure? It would seem, because of the punishment involved and the condemnation of mankind, even to the destruction of the race from the face of the earth, that this God is of a higher order than either the sons of God or the daughters of man. Certainly if God was only a saucerian or a visitor from outer space who had in some way participated in the development of man on this earth, He could not fault the improvement of the human race by the new-found relationship with other extraterrestrial visitors. Since many believe that the sons of God created man in the beginning by genetic manipulation, is it logical to believe they would destroy man for having relationships with their creator? Certainly one would not expect this to be so unless there was a serious moral problem involved in these actions.

Accepting the concept that there is a Supreme Being who created man and woman by His power and that these creatures disobeyed and fell into sin causing a fallen race may provide us with an answer to our dilemma. A fallen race of people, already marred by the sin of their disobedience, would likely enter into immoral relationships with other creatures. Therefore the fact that the relationship of the sons of God to the daughters of men was repulsive to God indicates that such depravity must be involved.

It is interesting to note that UFOlogists also claim to accept the Bible as literal truth and only attempt to reinterpret the Scriptures in light of saucer visitations. However, they seriously ignore other passages of the Bible, such as the great Flood mentioned in the later chapters of Genesis. This passage indicates that the God who was disturbed at the actions of man upon the planet Earth destroyed the earth by a great and migthy cataclysm of water covering the whole earth with water and mud. He destroyed all flesh. So great was the destruction that it was necessary to build a large boat in order to preserve life upon this planet. The story indicates that only one man and his family survived. The eighth verse of Genesis 6 tells us that only Noah found grace in the eyes of the Lord, that only Noah believed in the true Word of God and only Noah accepted the warning of judgment. This warning is clearly given in Genesis 6:3, right in the midst of the passage concerning the sons of God. For the Lord said that His Spirit shall not always strive with man, because man is flesh and his days would be numbered one hundred and twenty years. Here is a clear-cut warning which evidently was ignored. If, as UFOlogists tell us, it is necessary to accept the passage about the sons of God as literal, it seems equally necessary to accept the remaining portion of Chapter 6 as an historical event as well.

But what happened to the sons of God? Accepting the premise that they were visitors from some far-distant planet, they must have escaped to their planet with fear and trepidation. Or they were destroyed in this judgment and cataclysm. In any case there is strong evidence that there exists somewhere a being called "God" who is of a higher order than these extraterrestrial visitors. This God displays supernatural power over all physical entities, as displayed by His ability to destroy mankind by water and the great Flood. It is evident that the saucerians did not initiate the disaster of the Flood for even their own offspring were destroyed. This fact is interesting because of its implications to the future disasters predicted for the planet we inhabit.

We are now being warned of impending disasters. These disasters will not be caused by the saucerians. Is it logical then to deny the premise that there is a supernatural God and accept instead that God is only supertechnological? How does technology explain the destruction of the heavens and the earth? How does modern technology explain the creation of new ones? As the saucerians predict judgment and doom upon this earth as a fulfillment of the return of Christ, we again are faced with a dilemma. Are these saucerians proclaiming a false Christ and if so, what will happen to their followers when the true Christ is revealed? Considering the seriousness of this question let us evaluate the sons of God in a different light.

Traditionally it has been held that the sons of God were angels (which is fascinating considering that many saucerians claim they are messengers of God or angels). This is evidenced by the statement of Job 1:6 where the sons of God came to present themselves before the Lord. Job indicates that the sons of God came

before the true God known in this passage as the Lord.
This also occurred in Job 2:1. Here is a clear indication that the sons of God were subservient to a being
higher than themselves. From Job 38:7 we find that the
sons of God shouted for joy as the foundations of the
earth were formed, indicating that these beings are not
responsible for the creation of the earth but rejoiced at
the power and majesty of the God who was. In Job 1
and 2 Satan is indicated as being among the sons of
God. This is interesting since Satan was an angel. According to the Bible he was perfect in the day he was
created. The passage relates that the sons of God presented themselves to the Lord, Satan was indicated to
be one of them, and he was singled out because of specific conversations between the Lord and Satan concerning Job, an inhabitant of the earth.

As Satan revolted against God, usurping His authority, he gained the worship and following of man by
causing them to sin in the Garden of Eden. He convinced other angelic beings, sons of God, to follow him
in an open attempt to take over the earth. It is Satan
and his followers who control the hearts and minds of
sinful man, making it necessary for Jesus Christ, the
one and only Son of God, to lay aside His power and
die on the cross as a substitute for man's sin, so that
those who believe in His death and resurrection may
have eternal life in heaven prepared by God Himself.
But Satan is against man making this choice, in fact, he
is diametrically opposed to anything God stands for
and will use all of his power to deceive man into accepting other ideas.

It is not outside Satan's capabilities to attempt a
false fulfillment of the Biblical record, or even to attempt to deceive us concerning the power and nature of
God. Accepting the concept that the sons of God are
angels we gain a fuller understanding of the meaning of
the passage in Genesis 6.

The sons of God are males, as indicated by the term "son," and they took unto themselves wives of the daughters of man. The Bible clearly states that angels among themselves do not marry nor are given in marriage. This is because there are no female angels. As males these followers of Satan had relations with female descendants of a fallen Adam and Eve. When we realize that men are a little lower than angels and that man in his fallen condition is vastly different from the perfection God intended for man when He created him, we can understand why the children born were giants possessing great wisdom and stature. This also gives us great insight into the depravity of the entire human race. Since these fallen angelic beings were disrupting God's creation, it became necessary to destroy man in the great Flood. But angels themselves suffered punishment as 2 Peter 2:4–12 relates:

> For if God spared not the angels that sinned, but cast them down to hell, and delivered them into chains of darkness, to be reserved unto judgment;

> And spared not the old world, but saved Noah the eighth person, a preacher of righteousness, bringing in the flood upon the world of the ungodly;

> And turning the cities of Sodom and Gomorrah into ashes condemned them with an overthrow, making them an example unto those that after should live ungodly;

> And delivered just Lot, vexed with the filthy conversation of the wicked.

> (For that righteous man dwelling among them, in seeing and hearing, vexed his righteous soul from day to day with their unlawful deeds;)

> The Lord knoweth how to deliver the godly out of

temptations, and to reserve the unjust unto the day of judgment to be punished:

But chiefly them that walk after the flesh in the lust of uncleanness, and despise government. Presumptuous are they, self-willed, they are not afraid to speak evil of dignities.

Whereas angels, which are greater in power and might, bring not railing accusation against them before the Lord.

But these, as natural brute beasts, made to be taken and destroyed, speak evil of the things that they understand not; and shall utterly perish in their own corruption;

Peter is telling us that even angels that sinned are not to be spared and even with their power and might they do not dare to speak out against God.

Jude further emphasizes this fact in verses 6 and 7.

And the angels which kept not their first estate, but left their own habitation, he hath reserved in everlasting chains under darkness unto the judgment of the great day.

Even as Sodom and Gomorrah, and the cities about them in like manner, giving themselves over to fornication, and going after strange flesh, are set forth for an example, suffering the vengeance of eternal fire.

In this passage in Jude we are told there are angels bound in chains awaiting judgment. This indicates that the sinful acts and attitudes of those angels did not go unpunished. For, like the inhabitants of Sodom and Gomorrah who were destroyed for their lust after angelic beings, even powerful angels will be judged in eternal fire. Even today Satan still lives on this planet

and controls the lives and hearts of men with his great
deceptive powers. With his demonic followers he fills
our minds with thoughts of lust and greed and perverts
the true meaning of the Word of God, capitalizing
upon our reluctance to accept that which we cannot
explain. He constantly subjects us to false influences
and fulfillments of Biblical truth. Even in the temptation of Jesus Christ, in Matthew 4, Satan used the Bible
in an attempt to gain the worship of the only true Son
of God, but Christ resisted the temptation and gained
victory over Satan by His subsequent death and resurrection. By arising from the dead He demonstrated His
power over death and strengthened His statement that
those who believe in Him should be given eternal life.
Realizing this it is evident from the message of the saucerians, the new sons of God, that we are being deceived into a false fulfillment of the Biblical record. Yet
when we consider Christ's warning of signs and
wonders from the heavens and the proclamation of
false messengers from false Christs, the sons of God
are in reality simply fulfilling the Bible.

Before the birth of Christ, Satan and his followers
instigated the religion of Mithraism which required its
followers to repent of their sins and be baptized in
pools of blood. Thus before Christianity ever began to
be proclaimed there was already a counterfeit in existence. Many people refused to accept the idea of repentance from sins and baptism in water because of the
similarity to the dreaded cult of mythraism. And so
many people refused to believe the truth because of this
deception. It would seem that similar practices of deception are now being proclaimed as advocates of
UFOlogy tell us we must reinterpret the Bible in order
to explain visitations from outer space. It would seem
more logical that we ought to accept the Biblical record
and examine the record for similar types of deception

in order to fully understand the implications of the message of the saucerians.

Their motive, then, in proclaiming the return of Christ is to deceive humankind. Because the saucerians' fate is eternal damnation they want to take as many men and women with them as possible. Ultimately they hope to gain enough followers to attempt one final revolt. But even that revolt is predicted in the Bible and the results are already known.

SEVEN

The Problem

The remaining verses of Genesis 6 give strong evidence to support the concept that fallen angels participated in depraved acts with people in the days before the Flood. We are told in verse 11 that *all* flesh was corrupt. So horrid were these acts, so Satanic in their nature, that it was necessary for God to totally destroy the world with water, condemning some angels to an existence in chains as a warning for the future. There is strong evidence to support this concept that the whole world was totally destroyed with water in the not-too-distant past. Such a destruction lends credence to the reality of the Word of God in the life of the Christian and certainly acts as a strong warning of judgment to those who refuse to accept the Biblical record.

The Genesis account of the Flood describes in great detail the destruction which took place on a global basis (Genesis 7:17-24).

And the flood was forty days upon the earth; and the waters increased, and bare up the ark, and it was lift up above the earth. And the waters prevailed, and were increased greatly upon the earth; and the ark went upon the face of the waters. And the waters prevailed exceedingly upon the earth; and all the high hills, that were under the whole heaven were covered. Fifteen cubits upward did the waters prevail; and the mountains were covered. And all flesh died that moved upon the earth, both of fowl, and of cattle, and of beast, and of every creeping thing that creepeth upon the earth, and every man: All in whose nostrils was the breath of life, of all that was in the dry land, died. And every living substance was destroyed which was upon the face of the ground, both man, and cattle, and the creeping things, and the fowl of the heaven; and they were destroyed from the earth: and Noah only remained alive, and they that were with him in the ark. And the waters prevailed upon the earth an hundred and fifty days.

Note the essentials of the description: the waters prevailed, they were increased upon the earth exceedingly, all of the high hills under the heaven were covered, the water was so high that it covered the highest mountain by a distance of fifteen cubits (a cubit is approximately eighteen inches, so the waters were above the highest mountain some twenty-two and a half feet). Mount Ararat is sixteen thousand nine hundred and forty-six feet in elevation. Since water seeks its own level, if it was over seventeen hundred feet at Mount Ararat in Turkey, it would flood the Mesopotamian Valley and the desert, and it would inundate vast parts of Europe, Asia, and the rest of the world.

In verses 21–23 we are told that *all* flesh died which moved upon the earth—"cattle . . . beast . . . every creeping thing . . . and every man: All in whose nostrils was the breath of life, of all that was in the dry land, died. And every living substance was destroyed which was upon the face of the ground, both man, and cattle, and the creeping things, and the fowl of the heaven; and they were destroyed from the earth: and Noah only remained alive, and they that were with him in the ark." The text clearly denotes that all living things were destroyed except those inside the ark. Christ describes that event for us in Matthew's gospel (Matthew 24:37-39).

> But as the days of Noe were, so shall also the coming of the Son of man be. For as in the days that were before the flood they were eating and drinking, marrying and giving in marriage, until the day that Noe entered into the ark, And knew not until the flood came, and took them all away; so shall also the coming of the Son of man be.

Here the Lord Jesus uses the account of the universal Flood and its destruction to point to His second coming and judgment, which is also a universal event. As in the days of Noah, when all who were outside the ark were destroyed, so it will be at the coming of the Son of Man when all those outside the ark of safety, Jesus Christ (those who have not accepted Him as Saviour), shall be judged and condemned.

Look also at 2 Peter 3:6: "Whereby the world that then was, being overflowed with water, perished." The word "overflowed" in the Greek *(kataklusmos)* means "cataclysmized," and it signifies just that—a total cataclysm. Peter says that the world that then was, being overflowed with water, perished. That description is used in the New Testament only in reference to the Flood of Noah's day, not to a local or small flood, in which case another word is used (Matthew 7:25, *potamos*). This account tells us that *all* in whose nostrils was the breath of life and who were outside the ark were destroyed.

The Flood was all-inclusive. It did cover all the earth, it did cover all of the high hills under the whole heaven, and it did destroy all animal and plant life. And if there were such an event, we ought to find evidence of two things: 1) it was possible for Noah to build an ark that would accommodate his family and pairs of all land-dwelling animals; and 2) there must be geological evidence in today's world that such an event occurred in the past.

First of all, let us look at the size of the ark to see if the Biblical account is reasonable. In Genesis 6:15 we read, "And this is the fashion which thou shalt make it of: The length of the ark shall be three hundred cubits, the breadth of it fifty cubits, and the height of it thirty cubits." With a cubit of approximately eighteen inches, the ark was approximately four hundred and fifty feet long, seventy-five feet wide, and forty-five feet high. It was built in the shape of a giant rectangular box, more like a railroad boxcar than the ocean-going vessels of today. It did not include a rudder to enable Noah to steer it. The ark would have an extra-large capacity, float well, be exceptionally stable, and be capable of withstanding the Flood waters and the breaking up of the fountains of the deep. People who claim to have seen the ark of Noah resting on the mountaintop of Ararat report that there is a catwalk several feet wide down the center of the top with a row of windows under it and extending the entire length of the ark. The sixteenth verse says, "A window shalt thou make to the ark, and in a cubit shalt thou finish it above." Notice that it does not require one little square window in the top that is a cubit, but that "a cubit shalt thou finish it above." The roof was raised and has windows all along the side which possibly were used for trapping fresh water.

One question seems paramount: Is it possible for such a ship to hold all of the animals needed to preserve life upon the earth? Ernst Mayr, an outstanding taxonomist and evolutionist, offers an estimate of well over one million species of animals living on the earth today, and that does not include eight hundred and fifty thousand species of insects. It would obviously be impossible to place a million species of animals in the ark. However, if we analyze Ernst Mayr's figures as discussed in *The Genesis Flood,* by John C. Whitcomb and Henry Morris, we find that we can eliminate a large number of animals which could survive in the water. Noah did not have to take goldfish into the ark, nor did he build tanks for the piranhas or killer whales. The seventh chapter specifies that "all in whose *nostrils* was the breath of life, of all that was in the dry land"—man, cattle, creeping things, fowl of the heaven, every living substance—"was destroyed which was upon the face of the ground." Fish are not mentioned anywhere in that seventh chapter, so Noah did not have to account for fish, sponges, echinoderms, protozoa, and all other sea animals. For that matter, we could also eliminate amphibious animals who survive in the sea, but for the sake of argument we will account for these. Using Mayr's figures again, we need only seventeen thousand and five hundred species of animals to preserve life on *earth*. The preservation of life requires one male and one female, so now we need seventeen thousand and five hundred pairs of animals, or thirty-five thousand animals, in the ark.

One may immediately envision very large animals, such as elephants and giraffes, but most animals are smaller than sheep. In fact, the average size of all animals combined is about the size of sheep. Since God sent the animals to Noah, in His wisdom He probably supplied small young animals to be taken into the ark because they would live longer, survive the voyage better, and fulfill the purpose of continuing life on the earth. Taking into consideration that we are accounting for amphibious animals, we will also assume the animals were fully grown. Thirty-five thousand sheep can be placed in one hundred and forty-six railroad boxcars. In accounting for insects and creeping things, we will give insects two inches of flying room and, including creeping things, provide another twenty-one railroad boxcars. A total of one hundred and sixty-seven railroad boxcars, therefore, could accommodate the animal species living on the earth if we adopt Mayr's figures. Using the smallest cubit known, seventeen and one-half inches (though it may be as long as twenty-two inches), the ark had a capacity of five hundred and twenty-two railroad boxcars. This means that all of the animals in the ark could be placed on one of the decks, Noah and his family on another deck, and an entire deck remain for the bowling alley, badminton area, shuffleboard, and swimming pool. Or perhaps that space was used for animals which became extinct before out time.

What about some of the large extinct animals such as dinosaurs? Before we discuss the space they needed, let us discuss how dinosaurs are dated. When finding a dinosaur bone, a paleontologist looks at the rock strata from which the bone was taken and carefully examines the bone. He or she determines that the dinosaur is seventy million years old. But how does the paleontologist know the dinosaur is seventy million years old? This age is determined because the fossil appears in cretaceous strata which are believed to be seventy million years old. This fact is reported in all of our textbooks, all of our encyclopedias. Obviously anything found buried in rock laid down seventy million years ago had to be buried when that rock was formed and would have to be seventy million years old also. But how do we know cretaceous strata are seventy million years old? Because dinosaurs are found in it! Although this illustration is oversimplified, we are confronted with a classic example of circular reasoning. The fossil is dated by the rock in which it is found and the rock is dated by the fossil it contains.

Carl Dunbar, in his book on historical geology, admits the circular reasoning involved. A few years ago the *Encyclopedia Britannica,* in an article on fossil dating, made a statement that circular reasoning is indeed involved in the dating of fossils but since it is so consistent it must be correct! Actually, there is no accurate way to date a fossil. Carbon 14, granting all of its assumptions, is accurate back to about thirty thousand years. How can a seventy-million-year-old fossil be dated with a dating method only going back thirty thousand years? It can't, so scientists do not use Carbon 14 to date fossils.

Sedimentary strata are laid down by water; one can date them by finding an intrusion in the strata. If some lava flow, granite, or other type of igneous rock intrudes through the sedimentary strata, one can date the intrusion and know that the sedimentary layer above had to be laid down before the date of the intrusion. But since there is no accurate way to date the sedimentary rock, there is no accurate way to date the fossil. The geologic column, or fossil record, is built upon the assumption that evolution is true. The geologic column is established by accepting an evolutionary sequence for the fossils and by estimating the time required for one form to evolve to another. The picture of geologic history supposedly recorded in the geologic column is based upon the "fact" of evolution, which in turn is built on the "fact" of the geologic column. Again, circular reasoning is involved; neither item can be demonstrated or proved.

All we can really tell about dinosaurs and other large animals is that they lived sometime in the past. If you converse with the paleontologist who is digging at Dinosaur Monument in Vernal, Utah, he will tell you that the dinosaurs did not die in the park area, but were living upstate somewhere. They were crossing a sand bar or walking in a swamp and something happened, such as a local flood, that caused these dinosaurs to die. They were then washed downstream by water and buried in the sandstone at Vernal, Utah; they were both destroyed and buried by some type of water action. There is no way to tell when this event took place. Scientists can only state that dinosaurs lived sometime in the past and were destroyed sometime in the past by water action. This can easily be placed into a Biblical perspective.

The word "dinosaur" means "terrible lizard." A dinosaur is nothing more than a large reptile. But a reptile affords a most unusual growth phenomenon: the longer a reptile lives, the larger he grows. He is certainly not like man, who lives for twenty years growing upward and then (unfortunately) spends the rest of his life growing outward. If reptiles live for a hundred years, they grow for a hundred years. The Bible establishes the framework that God created animals, plants, and people and placed them in a perfect environment.

It was so perfect that even after people fell into sin, they lived nine hundred and thirty years before dying. The average life span during the time between creation and the Flood was nine hundred and eleven years, whereas our average life span today is about seventy years. We would have to increase our present life span some thirteen times to match the earlier life span. Increase the life span of a reptile proportionately, some thirteen times, and it is not too hard to picture how the iguana, growing for this period of time, could become large enough to look like a dinosaur. Picture the twelve-foot reptile living in China today and then increase his size and you will account for another of those gigantic reptiles that lived on the earth.

Consider also that in the pre-Flood world people were instructed to eat the vegetation. Before the Flood there were tremendous amounts of minerals and trace elements in the soil necessary to produce the vitamins and proteins needed for humans to gain all the nutrition necessary for life. Animals shared this same food. After the Flood these trace minerals no longer remained in the soil, but were washed out to sea. This may account for the fact that the largest animal living today, the whale, exists in the sea.

Ted Manthei has developed some interesting studies of the minerals in the sea. He has taken the trace minerals out of a lake bed, used this for fertilizer, and grown tomatoes larger than average. The fruits of these plants are disease resistant and bug free, with a lasting quality. They will eventually dehydrate and dry up, but they do not rot. Today man needs to take supplementary vitamins because there is not enough protein or minerals in the soil to enrich the vegetation. Before the Flood the earth had a tropical climate and mineral-enriched vegetation which were quite conducive to producing large forms of life.

How did these animals die out? The evolutionist has

about seventy different answers, which can be divided into some thirty-five categories. In fact, evolutionist answers are largely contradictory. The climate was too hot or too cold, there was too much food or not enough food, and so on. Yet it *is* agreed that if large fossils are buried in sedimentary strata, some type of water action was responsible.

When did these animals die out? In a river bed in Glen Rose, Texas, dinosaur prints are found in the same strata with human prints. Dinosaur eggs, or large reptile eggs, were found off the coast of Madagascar up to one thousand years ago. Cave paintings in Rhodesia show a brontosaurus painted by bushmen who are known to have left the caves about 1500 B.C. The interesting factor here is that the bushmen painted only things they could actually see. How then can we account for the painting of a brontosaurus unless one was actually seen living at that time (a much more recent dating than evolutionists allow)? Everett Purcell of the Creation-Science Research Center wrote to a paleontologist in Rhodesia and asked him about this. The reply was classic. He answered that obviously the painting could not be of dinosaurs because dinosaurs died out seventy million years ago (this conclusion was made without even going to view the paintings). The cave paintings must be either of giraffes or ant bears (an ant bear is a type of aardvark or anteater). We decided that any paleontologist who could not tell the difference between a giraffe and an anteater probably would not know a brontosaurus if he saw one! The point is, he would not even leave his office to investigate; his mind was made up.

If we reevaluate the position of the geologic column, the age of the earth, and even the position concerning the evolutionary bias, we can come up with better answers. The Biblical framework allows for dinosaurs: they would have been created in the Garden of Eden, died out or destroyed in the Flood, and buried in various sedimentary strata.

Why did these large animals die out? After the Flood the conditions that are necessary for longevity no longer existed. Even man's life span dropped to four hundred years, then to two hundred years at Babel; after another two hundred years, in Abraham's time, Sarah was too old to have children at age 90. Man's life span has been decreasing even since. (Incidentally, to-day's increase in life span does not mean that we live longer but that fewer children die at birth. The average life span in the United States is seventy years; in India it is only thirty-five years because more children die at birth in India than in America. People in India live as long as people in America, but the infant mortality rate lowers the average life span.)

The ninth chapter of Genesis says that the day Noah left the ark "the fear of you [man] and the dread of you shall be upon every beast of the earth, and upon every fowl of the air, upon all that moveth upon the earth, and upon all the fishes of the sea; into your hand are they delivered. Every moving thing that liveth shall be meat for you; even as the green herb have I given you all things" (verses 2-3). For the first time Noah is instructed to eat meat, and man and beast are now en-emies. This is necessary because the earth lacks the fo-liage and vegetation necessary to sustain man's life.

The fact that dinosaurs and other large animals are extinct is not an unusual problem. Over the years, many animals have become extinct—for instance, we are cur-rently in danger of losing the bald eagle, and man's destruction almost eliminated the buffalo. If it were not for our wild life and game preserves, many more animals would probably be extinct.

We often think of dinosaurs as being terribly fero-cious. Two evolutionary scientists in England who have done research on the tyrannosaurus rex and allosaurus conclude that both were vegetarians. The teeth are quite strong, suggesting a carnivorous animal, but the shape of the jaw and the nature of the upper arm is such that they would not be able to rip and tear, much less grab at their prey. The shape of the jaw indicates a tendency for them to lean upward and take things from a tree. Thus they do not seem to have been the ferocious animals we envisage. Few complete skeletons of dinosaurs are found, and thus our information is extremely limited. In fact, museum reconstructions and drawings in books may not give a true picture of the animals at all.

God told Noah to take all of His animals into the ark. Poor Noah—sitting with thirty-five thousand animals and eight hundred and fifty thousand species of insects. He and his family had to care and feed all of these animals for a year, which would certainly tax the strength of any individual. But observe one verse in passing—Genesis 8:1: "And God *remembered* Noah, and every living thing, and all the cattle that was with him in the ark." (Emphasis added.) That word "remembered" is an interesting word. Usually we think of remembering as recalling something we forgot. This definition would convey the idea that God was so busy destroying the whole earth that suddenly He looked down and remembered Noah was there. For an explanation of the term, we find a parallel in the New Testament. The thief on the cross said to the Lord Jesus, "Lord, *remember* me when you come into your kingdom." Was it only *after* the Lord died, was resurrected, and ascended into heaven that He thought, "I remember the thief on the cross"? Not at all. While still upon the cross He told the thief, "This day thou shalt be with me in paradise." He not only *remembered* but gave full assurance that He would take care of his need. This is what the Genesis text conveys. God remembered Noah, all the cattle, and every living thing that was in the ark, and He cared for their needs.

Many animals living today hibernate. Scientists, although they have studied these animals, cannot fully understand why animals hibernate, with some animals sleeping through the winter, some through the summer (called estivation), and living the whole time in a type of suspended animation. What is the reason for this? A close study of the Bible discloses that tropical conditions existed throughout the world before the Flood. There were seasons, but they were very mild, for it did not rain upon the earth before the Flood, and there was a tropical climate throughout the Earth so animals would not need to hibernate. Why do animals go into hibernation? To escape drastic seasonal changes. This is possibly a carry-over from the animals who were on the ark. God slowed down their metabolic processes to such a level that they spent their time in the ark in a state of hibernation. This would make it easier for them to survive the voyage and would simplify Noah's responsibility for them. There is good evidence from the text that such an event took place, because the Bible tells us that the animals entered the ark two by two and left the ark a year later two by two—including the rabbits. God's purpose, according to Genesis 8:17, was to preserve life so that after the Flood the animals could multiply and repopulate the earth, not the ark. It seems logical that God performed this miracle and slowed down the metabolic processes.

If a worldwide Flood occurred, we would expect to find evidence of animals and plants buried by some type of water action throughout the earth. We find this in sedimentary strata—strata which are laid down by wind or water. The entire geologic column is built of sedimentary strata, even some pre-Cambrian rocks. This type of strata are found in the Grand Canyon, which is one of the best areas of the earth to study because of the extensive series of strata exposed. A drastic change in strata is brought about by some type of water action. The historical geologist, the evolutionist, and the uniformitarian would explain this change as a gradual formation, a gradual laying down of the sediments, based on the present rate of sedimentation. If the rates of erosion and deposition were sufficiently increased, the Grand Canyon could be formed or eroded in a short period of time.

According to the Bible, the Flood was such that the fountains of the great deep were broken up. Throughout the ocean floor in the mid-oceanic ridges, a rift circles the entire earth. This suggests that some time in the past the ocean floor was uplifted about two miles, which would be enough to cause a flood and cover the entire land mass with water. There is enough water in the ocean even now to cover the entire earth if it were rearranged. A study of oceanography points to various places in the earth where water would have drained out; the easiest way to cause that drainage after the Flood would be to raise the land mass and the mountains. Estuaries, oceanic canyons, and underwater caverns which go back underneath the seashore are places where drainage and erosion have taken place. Visual evidence at Lake Bonneville today shows that in the past it covered a vast area. The mountains in that area have shorelines where the lake used to be. It has gradually subsided to the present level. Vast portions of land were under water, as shown by the evidences of fossils buried on the tops of mountains by water action. Even on Mount Ararat itself sedimentary strata are found at the thirteen thousand-foot level, an indication that water was at that level. Pillow lava, molten lava cooled under water, is found at the fifteen thousand-foot level on Mount Ararat. The conchoidal fractures indicate that it had to be cooled under water. Such illustrations are found everywhere on the earth's surface and offer good evidence for the global effects of water action.

Geology books tend to give the impression that the geologic column is found in the exact order traditionally proposed by historical geology. However, nowhere on earth are the strata laid down in exactly the same order as in the books. In the Grand Canyon, which is probably the best single area for investigation, over half of the geologic column is missing. Such an irregularity is usually explained as caused by unconformities. That is, erosion somehow wiped out the strata which are now missing in that area, and the next stratum was laid down, omitting the eroded layers of strata.

The same type of stratum is not always found directly lying on top of basement rock. Cretaceous rock, supposedly seventy million years old, is found lying right on top of basement rocks, and so is Cambrian rock, supposedly older than five hundred million years, or Permian rock, frequently dated at two hundred million years. In numerous places on earth strata have been found drastically out of order. At Chief Mountain, Montana, at the Lewis Overthrust, pre-Cambrian rock lies on top of the younger Cretaceous. A pre-Cambrian rock, according to evolutionary dating methods, would be over five hundred million years old. A Cretaceous rock would be seventy to one hundred million years old. This presents a slight problem: a rock which is over five hundred million years old is lying on top of one that is seventy million years old, four hundred and thirty million years are missing and the rocks are in an upside-down order. The evolutionist explains it quite simply: at one time all were level, but a horizontal thrust took place, forcing the strata to rise up, fold over, shear off all the adjacent strata, and leave this little pre-Cambrian block lying on top of the younger Cretaceous. Erosion washed away five hundred million years of strata above it, leaving a pre-

Cambrian block (thirteen thousand square miles in area) on top of a Cretaceous block.

In opposition to this, there is no real physical evidence of a thrust fault or a theory to explain the origin of the thrusts. There is no evidence of sliding, of pres-Owl's Head formation at Tortillita Mountains in Arizona and at other locations, evidence of small sure, of any rock movement between the two strata at the contact line between the two layers at Chief Mountain. In fact, the layer lies comfortably on top of the younger layer. In checking out overthrusts, such as the overthrusts clearly exists; up to forty feet of ground-up rock are found between the strata. At Chief Mountain three hundred and fifty thousand billion tons of rock must slide a distance of fifty miles in order to leave this block of pre-Cambrian strata on top of the Cretaceous, but there is absolutely no evidence of rock movement. Some say that you would not expect to find evidence of rock movement because it would be possible for the rock to slip in on a plastic flow and drop into place. But that is a theory without any physical evidence to support it. There is simply no evidence of such an event. Fossils are found out of order in the Swiss Alps, also. Some scientists suggest that at one time the Alps were in Africa and slid magically into Europe. At Chief Mountain, however, four hundred and thirty million years of geologic column have been done away with or reversed. All that can be deduced by looking at the geologic column and studying the fossils in any local area is that the stratum on the bottom was laid down before the stratum on top, unless one can find real evidence of thrusting, folding, or faulting. In the absence of such evidence it cannot be determined if the strata were laid down a week apart, two days apart, or a year apart.

If there were a worldwide Flood, we would expect to find evidence of the destruction of plants and animals on a large scale. For instance, to form a seam of coal in the earth one foot thick, about twenty feet of vegetation is needed, compressed adiabatically, that is, compressed under pressure without loss of the heat of compression. Theories for the formation of oil demand the burial of animal life on a large scale, again compressed adiabatically. If you were to bury me in the earth under the proper conditions and proper amount of pressure, supposedly you could come along later, stick a tube into me, pump me out, put me into your car, and drive down the street. The formation of coal and oil does not require millions of years, as the evolutionist sometimes claim, but can be accomplished in a relatively short period of time. Recently oil has been formed by converting a ton of garbage into a barrel of oil with the proper pressure and temperature conditions. In an hour and a half a piece of wood was converted to coal in Germany by using a pile driver. This was not their intention, but they applied the right amount of pressure and converted the material into coal. The proper amount of pressure determines the formation of coal or oil, not long periods of time.

When we compare the carbon to hydrogen ratio of the animal kingdom with the relationship of carbon to hydrogen in the plant kingdom, we find an interesting ratio. Compare the carbon to hydrogen content of oil to the carbon to hydrogen content of coal and one finds that the same ratios hold. This indicates that sometime in the past there was an event which destroyed one biosphere, or one total amount of animals and plants, in order to form the amounts of coal and oil found in the earth. When did such an event take place? As we drill into the earth and find oil, we discover that it is still buried under geostatic pressure, which in some places is three times greater than hydrostatic or fluid pressure. This means that overburdens of rock are on top of the oil, trapping it and causing the tremendous pressure. But the pressure would have dissipated if the

trap had been formed any longer than ten thousand
years ago. In fact, since oil is still found buried under
near-geostatic pressure, the indication is that it was
buried less than five thousand years ago! Further study
can be done in this area through a book entitled *Pre-
History and Earth Models,* by Melvin Cook, a Ph.D. in
chemistry from Yale. Oil was formed from all of the
animals buried on the earth at the time of the Flood.
Because we find oil under geostatic pressure, it is a
good indication that this burial took place sometime
less than ten thousand years ago—very much in agree-
ment with the Bible's four thousand to five thousand
year old date for the Flood.

If there were a worldwide Flood, we would expect to
find some record of flood traditions around the world.
Almost every major culture—Chinese, Indian, Greek,
Roman, Babylonian—possesses records and traditions
of a major flood. Some suggest it was a local flood, but
all relate that the entire area and civilization they knew
was destroyed. Their hero, whether his name was Ut-
napishtim or Noah, was instructed to build some type
of ark, or raft, and climb to the highest mountain. He
was to take his wife and all of his animals with him.
They were instructed to take all of their possessions
because there was to be a great Flood which would destroy the wickedness of the earth. The Chinese story
adds that after the Flood their hero got drunk and lay
uncovered in his tent. One of his sons went into the father's tent, saw his nakedness, and told the other two
sons. These sons, Charma and Japote, backed in and
covered their father. It tells of the subsequent judgment
of one of the sons and later talks about the building of
a tower to heaven.

Near the Fiji Islands a missionary was giving an account of Noah and the ark when one of the natives
jumped up and exclaimed, "That is exactly like our account. Our ancestor was instructed to build an ark and

take all of his family and animals into the ark. But your ancestors wrote your account down, so it is more accurate than ours, which has been passed on by word of mouth." Although by themselves these Flood traditions would not prove much, when coupled with the other evidences they certainly support the premise of a worldwide Flood.

There is even evidence that the ark built by Noah still remains on the Mount of Ararat. It was first sighted in 722 B.C. by Armenian farmers who climbed the mountain to get pieces of the ark to wear around their necks as amulets to protect their crops from flood damage. There have been over twenty-four reported sightings of this object buried in the ice on Mount Ararat in the last one hundred and seventeen years by over one hundred and eighty-six different people. Several expeditions have photographed the ark and taken measurements and there are even those who have claimed to have gone inside and report there are cages large enough for animals. On the side of the third compartment there is a carving in an ancient language of perhaps a ship's log. Wood had been found on the mountain as recently as 1969. One might ask what is so important about finding wood on a mountain? Mount Ararat is a volcanic cone, a lava-based mountain which is covered by an ice cap almost seventeen thousand feet in elevation. Buried in ice on top of a lava flow on a mountain where there are no trees or hardwood native to that mountain for two hundred miles are found handhewn timbers impregnated with a black substance. The wood is extremely hard and said to be cypress, a modern derivative of gopher wood. If these timbers are not from the ark, what is their source? According to the translation of the Sumerian cuneiform writing found on Mount Karada near the base of Mount Ararat among other ancient writings were these words: "When the waters were upon the earth God the word sewed the seed of the word into the water and the seed came to rest on the mountains of Ararat." When we add to these statements the fact that NASA photographs taken by satellite reveal an object at approximately the fourteen thousand foot level of the mountain, as was reported in newspapers all over the world in early 1974, we can see the importance of this great discovery. This is a strong indication that the rest of the Biblical record concerning the Flood must be true.

When we add to this the fact that fossils (the remains of animals and plants), buried in sedimentary strata (which is a rock formation formed by water), are found all over the world we again can see evidence of this great catastrophe, if we will only take time to examine it.

Here we have an account of eight people (Noah and his family) who believed the message of God and rejected the claims and activities of the sons of God on this earth nearly forty-three hundred years ago. The results of the wickedness and evil and moral depravity of the sons of God and daughters of man ended in the total global cataclysm from which only eight people survived.

Is it possible to begin again with only eight people and produce the present population? If there were a Flood, as recorded in the Bible, we should be able to determine from population statistics that it is reasonable to begin forty-three hundred years ago with eight people and produce the present population. This is even possible if we discount six of the people and begin exclusively with Mr. and Mrs. Noah forty-three hundred years ago. Suppose Noah and his wife lived forty-three years each. Suppose in addition that their children lived forty-three years and died, their children's children lived forty-three years and died, and that no overlapping generations existed. By these calculations, Noah would only see his children, not his grandchildren. Set-

ting it up this way gives us one hundred equal generations of forty-three years each between Noah and
today. The present average life span, of course, is seventy years, and most people live to see not only their
children but their grandchildren and some of their
great-grandchildren. Thus our conservative figures and
assumptions seem quite reasonable.

If only two children are born, the population will always be two—two people give birth to two people, the
parents die, and two people remain living. So we must
calculate two and a half people born every generation,
one and a quarter boys and one and a quarter girls.
Subtracting for each person that dies, the present population, roughly three billion people, can be produced
within the last forty-three hundred years. The growth
rate of this population is one half of one percent per
year. The present growth rate of the population is two
percent. Beginning with Mr. and Mrs. Noah and coming
to the present population in forty-three hundred years,
the growth rate would only be one-fourth of the present
growth rate. That allows for times of wars, famines, and
various plagues. The figures resulting from these conservative estimates coincide quite well with population
statistics at the time of Christ. Because the Biblical
framework fits the known data and explains the data, it
is a reasonable model.

What about the evolutionist? He says man has been
on the earth one million years—or perhaps eight million, or thirty million. But suppose man was here one
million years ago, and allowing forty-three years per
generation, two and a half children per generation, add
up all the generations and subtract for those people
who have died, and you will find the present population
of the world should number 10^{2700}. We would be required to pack people in every available inch of land
upon the earth, fill up all of the oceans, put people on
top of people until we have filled space up to the sur-

face of the moon, continue building space platforms and fill up our entire universe with people, using every available inch of space and continue piling people on top of people until we go out as far as our most powerful telescopes can see, four billion light years. Fill all that available space with people in every direction and we can account for only 10^{100} of people.

Evolutionists' figures would suggest that the population ought to be 10^{2700}. Decrease the amount of people born in each generation to 2.002 children per generation so that we produce the present population over the last million years and still we find that over three hundred billion people have lived and died. If this is true, where are the human fossils, the graveyards, the bones of all these people who have died over the last million years? They are not available. Human fossils are very rare. Thus the evolutionary model does not fit the known data at all. The only reasonable account that fits the known data of science exists in the Word of God—there was a universal cataclysm in the days of Noah.

Note the words of the Lord Jesus Christ as found in Matthew 24:37: "But as the days of Noe were, so shall also the coming of the Son of man be." He warned that at His second coming, man would be eating, drinking, giving in marriage, and being overly concerned with material things, as in the days of Noah. This was man's condition when the Flood came and destroyed them all. As we consider the importance of the study of creation and the Flood, we find that it declares God's right to judge the world. God is a God of mercy and of love, but He warns of impending judgment. What better way to warn the world than to demonstrate His right to judge the world—I created, I have the right to judge.

As judgment came in the past, destroying perhaps three billion people and saving only eight, another judgment is imminent. God's time of judgment will come. People today who reject Jesus Christ and say it is foolish to believe in the Bible will one day meet Jesus Christ as their judge. The One who had the power to create, the One who had the power to destroy, is the One who has the power to save. As eight people were inside the ark of safety in the days of Noah and found salvation, so also today people who are inside the ark of safety, Jesus Christ (those who have accepted Him as Saviour), will be saved from that judgment which is to come.

This is a strong warning to people living on this earth today that the message of UFOlogists and saucerians, a message which in reality is a message of the sons of God or angels who have returned to this earth, is not to be heeded. We are not to believe their teachings or claims unless we are bent on our own destruction. The clearcut evidence of the great Flood or destruction in the past and the fact that fallen angels are chained should act as a warning. Just as judgment took place in the past, judgment will take place in the near future. The heavens and the earth which exist now will pass away, but I firmly believe that just as the sons of God, these fallen angels and followers of Satan, led the inhabitants before the Flood into depravity and rejection of God that they will attempt to do the same in the day in which you and I live. These claims of saucerian visitation and the attempted reconstruction of the Bible by advocates of this new religion should be totally rejected by the Christian. In order to honestly answer their claims we need to further evaluate the evidence and history after the Flood in order to be familiar with the remaining fallacies in the arguments of those who worship saucerians.

EIGHT

---◆---

The Deception

UFOlogists would have us believe that all past civilizations are the result of saucer visitation upon this earth; that the glory of the Egyptian empire could not have been accomplished without the help of extraterrestrial visitors; and that the mighty pyramids of the Egyptians, Aztecs, Incas, and Mayans were all built under the supervision of intelligent beings from outer space. UFOlogists refer to artifacts which seem to be representative of saucer visitation. They look at carvings and paintings on rocks which they believe are ancient representations of space visitors. It is said that the truth of these visitations is obvious because people were not intelligent enough at that time to produce these great wonders and feats. After all, we are told, if our modern technology has difficulty explaining the building of these great pyramids then it is certainly necessary to call on outside forces in order to explain their existence. But is such a conclusion really necessary? Even though Satan lost a battle at the time of the Flood, he himself was not bound in chains. There were still many other fallen angels to do his bidding on the planet Earth. If Satan is now attempting to falsify the return of Christ by producing a counterfeit and appearing with his followers as extraterrestrial visitors, is it not logical to conclude that he used the same guise in the past? After all, each of these civilizations worshipped other gods instead of the one true God of the Bible. It would seem reasonable that as a minister of light, as a former prince of the power of the air, as a once powerful anointed angel of God who tempted man with the knowledge of good and evil, Satan possesses this power to deceive. Since he tempted Adam and Eve to follow him, plunging the entire race into sin and thereby obtaining their worship, it seems only logical that he would tempt other generations as well—that every descendant of Adam and Eve and those descendants of Noah after the Flood, would be tempted with knowledge. What better way to gain the worship of an empire than to appear to them in power, revealing himself as their god?

Let us not forget another possible explanation for these great buildings and artifacts, an explanation that is already found in the Bible. Let us not neglect the fact that Adam was created perfect and possessed all of the intelligence that is possible for man to have. Even after the fall his descendants were not primitive cavemen but were builders of cities and workers of metal achieving a highly developed civilization. Let us not forget Noah, a preacher of righteousness, yes, but also a builder of a great and mighty ark, a tremendous structure of great size which was adequate for the task of preserving life upon this earth. We have already mentioned the possibility of three billion people living on this earth with a high degree of technology. Is it not logical to conclude that Noah took with him the plans, writings, and the knowledge of all the civilizations that lived before the Flood? Such a conclusion is warranted by the activities of these eight people who survived that great destruction. Let us examine the Biblical record of events which took place after the great Flood.

From Genesis 9:19–29 we read of the curse of Canaan, which sheds some light upon the events of history.

These are the three sons of Noah: and of them was the whole earth overspread. And Noah began to be a husbandman, and he planted a vineyard: And he drank of the wine, and was drunken: and he was uncovered within his tent. And Ham, the father of Canaan, saw the nakedness of his father, and told his two brethren without. And Shem and Japheth took a garment, and laid it upon both their shoulders, and went backward, and covered the nakedness of their father; and their faces were backward, and they saw not their father's nakedness. And Noah awoke from his wine, and knew what his younger son had done unto him.

And he said, Cursed be Canaan; a servant of servants shall he be unto his brethren. And he said, Blessed be the Lord God of Shem; and Canaan shall be his servant. God shall enlarge Japheth, and he shall dwell in the tents of Shem; and Canaan shall be his servant. And Noah lived after the flood three hundred and fifty years. And all the days of Noah were nine hundred and fifty years: and he died.

Many people believe that this passage explains the origin of races. They suggest that the Negro comes from Canaan because the black color was his curse. But notice two things: verse 22, "And *Ham* the father of Canaan," and verse 24, "And Noah awoke from his wine, and knew what his *younger son* had done unto him. " (Italics added.) It was Ham who saw his father and Ham who told his two brothers. Yet Noah says, "Cursed be Canaan." Why?

Ham was not involved in some gross immorality. The Bible simply states that Ham, the father of Canaan, saw the nakedness of his father. The other two sons, Shem and Japheth, took a garment and, walking backwards, covered their father, not observing his nakedness. Prior to this action Ham evidently walked in, saw his father, came out, and said, "Look at our dad. He has been telling us that we ought to be good boys, yet he is in there drunk." This was not an act of immorality on Ham's part, but one of disrespect.

Who is Canaan? In the tenth chapter of Genesis we find that Canaan is the youngest son of Ham. Why was he cursed? The answer, in accord with Jewish custom, is suggested in 1 Samuel. When David slew Goliath, Saul asked, "Whose son is this that I may honor him?" Saul knew who David was, for David had played the harp for him—in fact, Saul had offered David his armor. But now Saul wanted to bless David for his great victory over the Philistines. How did he do it? By blessing Jesse, David's father. By laying blessing and honor on the father, Saul blessed the son. Likewise, when Joseph blessed Ephraim and Manasseh, he also blessed himself. Blessings go back one generation—and this would be equally true of a curse. Had Noah cursed Ham, he would be placing that curse upon himself. Yet he wanted to curse Ham and all his descendants, so he placed the curse on the youngest son of Ham, which reverts back a generation, covering Ham and all of Ham's children. This also eliminated Shem and Japheth from the curse.

In review, Noah could not have cursed Ham without cursing himself and bringing that curse upon his whole family, so in order to curse Ham he cursed Ham's youngest son, Canaan, who would have the same background, interests, and material-mindedness as his father. The curse of the youngest son Canaan covers all his brothers and comes back a generation to his father Ham, but it protects the two other sons of Noah.

What is the curse?

The curse is a prophecy. Realizing Ham's attitude, that he was not one who would honor his father, Noah says, "a servant of servants shall he be unto his brethren." Some people interpret "servant of servants" to mean a slave. But note other similar Biblical expressions. The Lord God is Lord of lords, which means He is the highest Lord of all lords. He is King of kings, the highest King of all kings. Paul says he was a Hebrew of the Hebrews, one of the highest Hebrews because he was of the tribe of Benjamin, one of the two tribes of the southern kingdom who remained true to Jerusalem and did not revolt. "A servant of servants" simply means the highest of all servants, not a slave. Because of Ham's mental attitude, Noah realized he was materialistically minded. A glance at the descendants of Ham will demonstrate that "Cush begat Nimrod: he began to be a mighty one in the earth. He was a mighty hunter before the Lord: wherefore it is said, Even as

Nimrod the mighty hunter before the Lord. And the beginning of his kingdom was Babel . . . . Out of that land went forth Asshur, and builded Nineveh." (Genesis 10:8–11). These people built cities. You do not find that attributed to the descendants of Shem or Japheth. Noah realized the implications of the mind of Ham, concerned with material things, and knew that Ham's children would also take up that attitude and interest. A pioneer who builds a city does not have time for reading, education, and luxuries—not even time to study the things of God. So the curse here is upon a materialistically minded people.

The Bible never mentions the word "race," which is a manmade term. Instead, the Bible speaks of nations. A careful study of history reveals that the descendants of Ham are those who have built the major cities—the Egyptians, Phoenicians, Babylonians, and Assyrians. These were the first major empires. The curse is not a curse of color, for color is nothing more than a genetic variation. Why do brown, white, and black rabbits exist? They are produced by a genetic variation, as do varied eye colors or the colors of flowers. The different skin colors of people on this earth are simple genetic variations.

The descendants of Ham, steadily concerned with materialistic things, have provided human beings with all the major technologies. Dr. Arthur Custance, an anthropologist in Canada, states that from the descendants of Ham we can trace most of the technologies of mankind with few exceptions. The airplane has been traced to them, the toothbrush, writing, arithmetic, ship building, and many other inventions which we consider part of our civilization.

By contrast, the descendants of Shem are concerned with spiritual things. The Bible says, "Blessed be the Lord God of Shem; and Canaan shall be his servant." The descendants of Shem include the Israelites or Jew-

ish people. They had the responsibility of taking the
message of God to the world, but they failed. The Lord
God originally planned to present His message to the
high priest, who would then pass it to the Levite priest;
he would then give it to the twelve tribes who would
pass it on to the world. But Israel kept that message to
themselves, and thus God found it necessary to go to
the Gentiles.

"God shall enlarge Japheth, and he shall dwell in the
tents of Shem." Traditionally the sons of Japheth have
been the ones concerned with the intellectual and philosophical things. They do not invent much, but they
improve on someone else's invention once it is given to
them. "By these were the isles of the Gentiles divided
in their lands; every one after his tongue, after their
families, in their nations" (Genesis 10:5). The descendants of Japheth (the Gentiles) at the time of Christ
were given the responsibility of presenting the message
of Christ to the descendants of Ham and Shem.

Thus there is one race—the human race—all descendants of Noah, all concerned with different things
because there are various individuals comprising this
race. You will find this true today.

At Babel a tower was built, resulting in a judgment
and a scattering of the nations. Until the time of Babel
there was something like a melting pot of people. One
had a choice of marrying a descendant of Japheth,
Ham, or Shem, all of whom lived near the one community. At the tower of Babel and immediately after-
wards, the people scattered and burst into seventy nations (Genesis 11), spreading themselves over the face
of the earth.

A family goes to one area and begins to build a civilization. They are similar in appearance, for by heredi-
ty children tend to look like their parents. The children
only know what they are taught, which, they, in turn,
teach their children. The descendants of Ham begin to

build cities. Later the descendants of Shem capture these cities. The descendants of Japheth do not accomplish much until they improve upon the other civilizations. Those who stay close to the cultural center continue to learn and develop. Those who pioneer and go farther away become less cultured and less civilized. As people move farther and farther away, back into areas such as Africa, they carry less and less civilization with them. Being hunters, like their father Nimrod, they develop cultures based upon hunting. This does not mean that they are any less intelligent because they are hunters.

Claude Lévi-Strauss, a leading evolutionary anthropologist, finds no evidence that man is any less intelligent in one area of the world than in another. In the most primitive cultures intelligence is the same. There is no evidence of the evolution of the human mind. So-called primitive tribes living in remote areas have complex languages and cultures. After they quit pioneering, settle down, and build their cultures, then perhaps they think about God. Only they do not remember the God who told them about the Flood; they do not remember the God of Noah. But they know there is a God and thus begin to set up a religion because they see other people establishing religions. Accounts of the past have been handed down by word of mouth. Eventually someone decides to write down all these accounts and traditions. Instead of having an account of the Flood, they come up with the Gilgamesh epic or a Babylonian epic. These have some truth in them but have been perverted by time. The farther away people get from the original center of civilization, the greater the tendency to create variants. We find, however, in all of the ancient tribes, all of the so-called primitive tribes, very strong cultural behavior. They are really not primitive; we merely consider them so because we compare them to our technical standards.

Anthropologists repeatedly point to the discovery of skulls representing primitive man, with the shape of the skull apparently reflecting its age. They seem to forget the effects of the environment and diet upon the shape of the human skull. Feed a child a diet in which he has to chew a great deal and the shape of the skull is formed accordingly. Feed another child all soft foods and the skull is formed quite differently. Deficiencies in vitamins and minerals likewise cause changes in the shape of the bones and of the skull. It is a mistaken idea to assume that the uglier the skull looks, the more primitive it is. The shape of the skulls considered in this writing have the look of primitiveness with ridges and extensions of the brow, but these could be accounted for on the basis of dietary deficiency as well as effects of the environment.

The Bible specifically mentions these characteristics of the sons of Noah and indicates that civilization would again begin in this cultural center around Ararat. As people dispersed from this cultural center they began to lose many of the benefits of civilization. As if to emphasize this fact the book of Genesis continues with an event which causes mass migration and could explain the origin of civilizations and primitive people throughout the world. In Genesis 11:1–9 we read:

And the whole earth was of one language, and on one speech.

And it came to pass, as they journeyed from the east, that they found a plain in the land of Shinar; and they dwelth there.

And they said one to another, Go to, let us make brick, and burn them throughly. And they had brick for stone, and slime had they for mortar.

And they said, Go to, let us build us a city and a tower, whose top may reach unto heaven; and let us make us a name, lest we be scattered abroad upon the face of the whole earth.

And the Lord came down to see the city and the tower, which the children of men builded.

And the Lord said, Behold, the people is one, and they have all one language; and this they begin to do: and now nothing will be restrained from them, which they have imagined to do.

Go to, let us go down, and there confound their language, that they may not understand one another's speech.

So the Lord scattered them abroad from thence upon the face of all the earth: and they left off to build the city.

Therefore is the name of it called Babel; because the Lord did there confound the language of all the earth: and from thence did the Lord scatter them abroad upon the face of all the earth.

Here is the account of the building of the tower of Babel. Notice the specifics of the account as these people have the ability to make brick, to burn them, and to manufacture mortar. They attempted to build a great city with the tower—all of the people speaking the same language, working together on this great project to build a tower into heaven. But God knew their purpose and He judged them and scattered them upon the face of the earth. Not only did the Lord confuse and scatter the people but He confounded their language so that they could no longer communicate with one another. No longer could they gather together for a common purpose that was outside of God's will. The people chose to build a tower to gain access to heaven rather than to obey God and find the realities of heaven through their faith and belief in God's Word. Let us not neglect one aspect of this which could possibly explain the building of civilizations throughout the world. In Genesis 10 we read that a man named Eber had two sons; ". . . the name of one was Peleg; for in his days was the earth divided; and his brother's name was Joktan." (verse 25). It is interesting to note that of all the names listed in this genealogy only the name of Peleg is qualified with the statement "for in his days was the earth divided." Peleg was born after the Flood and before the tower of Babel judgment. He lived during the tower of Babel judgment and was still alive after the judgment itself.

Is it not interesting that a man named Peleg, whose name means physical division, lived during the era of the tower of Babel? It would seem logical that this physical division refers to a dividing of the land mass which would also divide the nations. Many scientists are now talking about continental drift and ocean spreading, the concept that the continents themselves are moving away from each other. Some authorities are still highly critical of the theory, and as yet no one has proposed a satisfactory mechanism or an adequate driving force for the process. But could it be that when God scattered the nations, confounding their language, He also divided the continents so that man could no longer return to the area of Babel? Such a conclusion does seem logical and sheds some interesting light upon the problems of advanced civilizations starting up simultaneously around the world. For here a group of master builders with the knowledge to build great cities were scattered in the midst of a joint project, an attempt to build a tower to heaven. These people, who possessed extensive knowledge and the art of building, were divided and forced to migrate to new areas of the earth. In each of these new areas they built cities. Some of their cities contained great majestic pyramids. Such a premise explains the similarities of these structures to each other although they were built in distantly separated areas of the earth. The knowledge and intelligence Noah carried with him through the Flood, passed on to his descendants (especially through his son Ham), was now carried throughout the earth after the dispersion at Babel. It is interesting to note that the mythologies of various cultures tell of a lost continent of Atlantis. Could any of these legends refer to this great civilization where all of the nations of the earth were one before the great judgment of Babel? These legends would find their basis of fact in the destruction of this great city. Vast rifts filled by spreading seas separated the land mass and the people fled the destructive forces of this judgment. Since a map of the hypothetical continent of Pangaea (the name given to the one-continent world by scientists who believe in continental drift) centers around the present Middle East, the location of this cultural center, we find strong support that gives merit to this conclusion. The intelligence of Adam passed on to Noah, the intelligence and technology of a whole civilization destroyed in the Flood was carried on to his descendants by Noah and his family. Civilization, city building, was carried on by the people who were dispersed after the judgment of Babel. Of course, those who chose to hunt rather than to build scattered into their own areas, developed their own communities and hunting cultures, and soon lost the ability to build cities. As these master builders and master hunters died their knowledge was imparted to their offspring who in turn imparted it to their descendants as a civilization was built or a hunting empire was established. The need for building and establishing empires soon vanished. Men were left with the task of maintaining the civilization or culture that had been established and ultimately the knowledge and techniques used in building these great cities died. As techniques were lost, the civilization crumbled. Add to this, the fact of man's inherent nature to war against his neighbor, the effects of famine and plague, and we can realize the devastating results of death as it takes its toll on the civilizations of the past.

As we consider this interpretation of Biblical and archaeological data, let us not forget the depravity of man and his insistent worship of entities, spirits, or gods that are not the true God of the Bible. Civilizations have risen but they have also fallen and their fall and decline is linked with the depravity of their people and the rejection of God and their progressive moral decay and ultimate demise. It is fascinating to note that the nation Israel is the only nation that is promised that the greatness and glory of its kingdom will be restored as their King, the Lord Jesus Christ, returns to establish His rule over the earth.

The events leading up to the rapture of the church, the judgment of nations, and the return of Christ to set up His kingdom and reign for one thousand years demonstrate that the reality of this promise is close at hand.

The Satanic entities posing as angels and ministers of light are deceiving people in these last days. In an attempt to destroy the pure and life-giving message of the Bible they have come as visitors from outer space. But please remember, there is no scientific, empirical evidence for the existence of any being living outside our solar system. Photographs of Mars and Mercury reveal the impossibility of life in our solar system, so Satan is using this deception to fool and gain control of the population of this earth. Just as in the days before the Flood the sons of God participated in the corruption of all flesh in order to deceive man into the acceptance of the reality of the judgment which was to come,

Satan and his followers today are perpetrating this fraud upon humankind to attempt this false fulfillment of Biblical prophecy in order to neutralize faith in the true God.

But we who realize that the defeat of Satan is firm certainly ought to reject these claims of Satan. For today we can openly see the need for this admonition as we note the rise in satanic worship which is so prevalent in our society. Demonism is becoming increasingly popular and no longer can it be relegated to the realm of myth and fairy tales. Books and films like *The Exorcist* indicate the pain and torment of demonic possession and reveal the need for the power of Jesus Christ.

Witchcraft is practiced openly in the marketplaces of America and the world. At almost any newsstand one can purchase the necessary materials for performing occult rituals. There is even the organized Church of Satan, which openly practices demonic activities in opposition to the Word of God. As hard as it is to understand man's insistent need to worship and to study the supernatural, it is even more difficult to believe that man would choose to worship Satan, the god of this world, rather than the true God who ultimately possesses the victory. Perhaps this is due to man's denial of God and His power; perhaps it is due to the fact that he insists on worshipping himself. Impressed with his own knowledge and intellect, he places the creature above the Creator. It is in this that Satan may find his strongest ally. Capitalizing on man's greed and lust and desire for material pleasures and power, Satan gains his authority. There is even a Satanic bible so that followers of this dreaded cult can gain understanding of the ways of the prince of darkness. Demonic possession and Satanic worship are real, but they are not the total answer. Newspaper accounts and other documented reports indicate there is still a higher power, that as in the Biblical records demons will flee the power of Jesus Christ. One has only to read the daily paper for countless examples of the fulfillment of the Biblical statements concerning the casting out of demons. If there is a power higher than these demons and if people, using the power of Jesus Christ, can destroy the Satanic hold on an individual, is it logical to worship the demons? If Satan can be destroyed by the power of God, is it not foolish to place our trust in Satan? Satan is the great deceiver and many will follow his deception, but still we have the choice. Since the saucerians proclaim the coming of Christ in an attempt to deceive would it not be better to follow the true Christ who has sovereign power over all of these entities?

NINE

The Result

In order to understand fully the devastating effects of UFOlogy on historical Christianity, it is necessary for us to examine Biblical statements concerning Christ. As the Son of God, Jesus Christ came to this earth to die for the sins of mankind in order that people would be restored to the state of perfection they held before the fall. Our salvation is based solely and entirely on the death of Christ. The sufficiency of Christ's death rests completely on the dignity of His person. For this reason the importance of the study of the work and person of Christ cannot be overstated. It is the very heart of the Christian faith. Ultimately the acceptance or rejection of the fundamental Biblical doctrines concerning Jesus Christ will determine our eternal destiny. To reject these truths is to reject the person of Christ and to reject Him is to be lost, to be condemned to an eternity of misery and suffering. Therefore it is easy to see that the claims of the saucerians concerning the person of Jesus Christ in reality condemn the saucerians themselves. Jesus Christ is not a saucerian, He did not come to this planet in a flying saucer, He is not the offspring of a supertechnological, extraterrestrial visitor from the unknown regions of space. Jesus Christ is God.

He did not come into existence at the incarnation (His birth in a Bethlehem stable); He existed and acted previously to His coming to earth as a man. Christ has existed for all eternity. John 1:1 and 2 emphasize the fact that the Word was with God in the beginning and that the Word was equal with God. Christ has existed as long as the world everlasting, as stated in Micah 5:2 and John 8:58 where we find the statement "Before Abraham was, I am." Such a position is demanded because Christ is given the office of Creator and all things were expressly made by Him, a fact which indicates His earthly power (John 1:3; Col. 1:16). In addition, the Bible expressly calls Christ God (John 1:1, 1:18, 20:28; Titus 2:13; Heb. 1:8; 2 Peter

1:1; 1 John 5:20). One cannot deny the Biblical premise that Christ is God unless one is willing to reject these clear-cut statements regarding Christ.

Christ possesses the ability to forgive sins, as evidenced in Matt. 9:2 and 6 and to raise the dead (John 6:39, 40). He and He alone will execute judgment (John 5:22, 27). He accepted the worship of man, which indicates His equality with God (Matt. 15:25, 28; John 20:28). In addition to the fact that He is Creator of the heavens and the earth we find that He is also the Upholder and Sustainer (Heb. 1:3; Col. 1:17). He alone possesses the power that holds the universe together. Is it reasonable then to reject these Biblical claims concerning Jesus Christ in light of the fact that the Bible is so specific concerning His holiness? Certainly we should suspect the claims of the saucerians and wonder at the motive as we realize their strong deviation from proper Biblical interpretation.

Because of His love for mankind which He had created in the beginning, it was necessary to lay aside his godly attributes and return to the earth as a man. Living a sinless life He came to confirm His Father's promise to Eve that a Redeemer would come to save the world from the sinful state caused by Adam and Eve's rejection of God's word. He came to reveal the Father's will, to put away sin, and to destroy the works of the devil. By living a sinless life He gave us an example to follow in order that those who believe might be prepared for His second coming. As a man Christ could die on the cross. It was necessary for Him to experience death in order to be a substitute for our sins as described in Romans 5, 6, and 7. As a man Christ destroyed the curse placed on Adam's race and returned man to the state of righteousness that God intended for His creation. But this was only possible because Christ was also God and so His sacrificial death on the cross was accepted by God the Father in order that those who believe will forever have eternal life. His resurrection demonstrates His power over death and assures those who choose to follow in His footsteps and believe in His blessed name that they too will one day rise from the dead to be with Him throughout eternity.

At present, having ascended into heaven, Christ sits at the right hand of the Father, where He awaits the final judgment of the earth that is to come in the near future. Soon He will return to the earth to take the true believers to heaven with Him. After a period of seven years He will return to this earth in triumph and set up His kingdom for one thousand years. After this thousand years of peace Satan, who has been chained, will be loosed for a season and there will be a final revolt. Ultimately all who have rejected the name of Christ will be judged before the Great White Throne and will receive their final reward. These claims cannot be denied if one seriously considers the Biblical record.

Christ Himself predicted that false christs would come in the final days and He warned us to beware (Matt. 24:4, 5). The advocates of UFOlogy, in their attempt to substitute a supertechnological god for the supernatural God of the Bible, are simply fulfilling this prediction of Christ's. When we realize that the future of this earth is already known and has adequately been presented to us in the Bible, we can again see the futility of accepting the concept that Christ will return in a flying saucer.

The book of Revelation predicts the future events on this planet Earth. Beginning with the sixth chapter it describes a period of time known as the "great tribulation." This is a seven-year period of trials and tribulations for mankind. Directly preceding this period of tribulation believers in Jesus Christ are promised that they will be raptured (a term used to describe the taking away of followers into heaven to be with their

Lord). The tribulation period is characterized by three successive series of judgments. The first series begins with the opening of the seven seals of a special book in heaven. Only Jesus Christ has the power and authority to open this book because He was the Lamb who was slain for the sins of humankind. The events described below prepare humans for the final judgment before the righteous judge, Jesus Christ. At the opening of the first seal (Rev. 6:1-2), a dictator is revealed riding on a white horse going forth to conquer. This dictator is revealed as a Satanically controlled and possessed individual known as the antichrist or false Christ. Ultimately he will be recognized as the sovereign leader of the entire world for he will conquer the people of the earth. It is believed by experts that this person, who will soon be revealed, is alive today.

When the second seal is opened (Rev. 6:3-4), it reveals a rider on a red horse and denotes a period of war and bloodshed. It is here that Russia, with her Arab allies, will invade the Middle East and attack Israel. This war will ultimately involve all the major powers of the earth and lead to the great and final battle of Armageddon. This war will break out in the middle of this seven-year tribulation period, thus ending the period of peace.

At the opening of the third seal (Rev. 6:5-6), we find there is economic disaster. Famine is the true meaning of the rider on the black horse. Hunger and starvation will add fuel to the war that will be raging.

The rider on the pale horse, as revealed by the opening of the fourth seal in Rev. 6:7, stands for death and hell. Here we have death on a massive scale along with pestilence and plagues. These four horsemen indicate a disastrous world to come. They predict war on a global basis.

The opening of the fifth seal (Rev. 6:9-11), reveals a picture in heaven of believers in the true God who found their belief after the rapture and during this tribulation period. The souls of these martyrs cried out to God for deliverance. They were promised that at the end of the tribulation period they would be taken into heaven. True believers will be easy to identify during this period because they will refuse to wear the mark of the beast (the number 666) and thus will be prohibited from buying and selling. Rev. 14:9–11 warns of the destruction by the eternal God of those who receive this mark. It is, therefore, easy to see why those who refuse to wear it will suffer at the hands of the antichrist.

The opening of the sixth seal in Rev. 6:12–17 finds a tremendous earthquake, perhaps the greatest that has ever taken place on this earth. This quake may be caused by the first great nuclear exchange by the nations engaged in the violent war on earth. Perhaps now we can gain some insight into the warnings of the saucerians to lay aside our nuclear weapons. They realize that this event is predicted by God and will lead to their own destruction. What better way to attempt to stop that warfare than the insistent warnings against nuclear weapons? But, like the Flood that took place in the past, the events that take place in the book of Revelation assuredly will take place. This tribulation period is in reality a purging of the nation of Israel as it returns to belief in the true God.

Between the opening of the sixth and seventh seals we are told that there will be one hundred and forty-four thousand Jewish evangelists who proclaim God's true message to those who remain on the earth. This is to be a time and period of great global cataclysms and disasters.

At the opening of the seventh seal (Rev. 8:1–6), there is again a violent earthquake. So great is the judgment to come as a result of the opening of this seal that there is silence in heaven for one-half hour. When

this seal is opened it reveals to us a series of seven
judgments as indicated by the blowing of seven trumpets. As each trumpet is sounded drastic judgments
occur on the face of this planet Earth. As the first
trumpet is heard (in Rev. 8:7), there is a picture of
hail and fire mingled with blood. One-third of the trees
are destroyed and all grass is burned. This is a result of
a second great nuclear holocaust as the earth continues
this massive warfare.

The second trumpet indicates destruction upon the
water. It shows a massive hydrogen bomb explosion
causing the destruction of sea creatures as one-third of
the sea becomes blood (Rev. 8:8–9). One-third of all
ships will be destroyed as this nuclear havoc continues.

The third trumpet (Rev. 8:10–11) indicates the
contamination of one-third of all the fresh water supplies on the earth. A great many people will die as a
result of this poisoned water and the pollution will be
terrible. Although the water sources will be greatly affected, the atomic fallout of this great nuclear explosion will pollute our atmosphere even more, causing
one-third of the earth to be in darkness. This is indicated by the blowing of the fourth trumpet in Rev.
8:12. And still, in spite of all of the destruction around
them, men continue in this great battle bent upon their
own destruction. They are even warned of the foolishness by an angel (Rev. 8:13) who cries out three woes
upon the inhabitants of the earth. By refusing to believe people will suffer greatly from the three terrible
judgments that are to come. For at the blowing of the
fifth trumpet (Rev. 9:1–11) a terrible power is unleashed from the very pits of hell. Demons come to the
aid of Satan in this great attack upon humankind.
These demons will be in the form of locusts and will
have a leader called the Destroyer. They will unleash
painful torment on people, stinging them so badly that
they will wish they were dead.

The sixth trumpet (Rev. 9:12–19), which is actually the second woe, indicates a terrifying judgment with one-third of the population of the earth being destroyed by a mighty army of two hundred million Red Chinese. Entering into the battle with their allies they add to the total thermonuclear destruction of the earth as we now know it. Even in the midst of all that has been prophesied people still refuse to believe. So engrossed in the religions of this world and so deceived by the false statements of the antichrist and his prophet, people will continue in their sin and rebellion against God as indicated in Rev. 9:20–21. Clinging to worship of demons and idols, and to belief in the occult, man seems bent on his own destruction.

Before the blowing of the seventh trumpet, the final woe, there is a brief time of peace near the end of the tribulation period in which human beings are given a chance to return to God. There are many other events which will take place during this period of tribulation. Despite all of the warnings and opportunities to repent people, in their continuing insistence on rejecting the true God and following the antichrist, will lead to their final doom. Satan will be in full control during this period having deceived men and established his false prophet, who may be masquerading as Christ as predicted by the saucerians. Many people may believe that this false Christ returned in a saucer. This belief may give us some understanding of the basis for the influence awarded these beings as a result of the present warnings about extraterrestrial visitors. Believing in them, man will help to place them into authority and will believe and follow these antichrists and will eventually reject the true message of God.

During this period of trial and tribulation on the earth there will also be a great warfare taking place in heaven as the powerful angels of God battle the Satanic hosts. In Rev. 12:7–10 Satan and his followers fail in their last-ditch attempt to take over the kingdom of heaven and Michael, the great archangel, and his angels defeat Satan and cast him down to the earth. This then explains the total reign of terror by Satan upon mankind as he realizes the end is near. Thus Satan, called the "great dragon," centers his attention and attacks on the nation of Israel in a final attempt to destroy those who keep the commandments of God and the testimonies of Jesus Christ (Rev. 12:13–17). Many believers in Christ will be persecuted or slain during this time of tribulation. This may be the cause of the final doom and destruction placed upon Satan and his followers at the outbreak of the last great woe.

At the blowing of the seventh trumpet we find not one judgment but a series of seven as represented by the pouring out of seven vials of wrath. It is here that the final preparations for the greatest battle of all time are set. For in Chapter 16, verse 2, we learn that the first vial produces the most painful suffering that people have ever had to bear. There are sores inflicted upon all those who wear the mark of the beast and have chosen to worship him. In the third verse a vial or bowl is poured into the sea, which becomes the blood of dead men and every living thing in the sea will die. It is here that God begins to purge the evil forces of man and beast off the planet earth and demonstrates His power to all that they may believe. The rivers and fresh waters of the earth receive the third vial in Rev. 16:4–7 and they also become blood. Now those who have shed the precious blood of the believers in Jesus Christ will have nothing but blood to drink.

The fourth vial is poured upon the sun and increases its intensity so that people living on the earth are scorched with great heat. Still they blaspheme God and refuse to believe (Rev. 16:8–9).

As the fifth angel pours out his judgment upon the throne of the beast his kingdom becomes darkness.

This may allow the armies of the world to gather and converge on this revived Roman empire and prepare for the final destruction which will take place in the Middle East.

The sixth angel pours his bowl upon the great river Euphrates which dries up in order to prepare for the final battle of Armageddon (Rev. 16:12–16). It is here that unclean spirits like frogs come out of the mouth of the dragon, out of the beast, and out of the false prophet. Then these spirits of demons go forth and work miracles for all the kings of the earth in order to gather them into this one place for the final battle. Every army of the world will be gathered into a great coalition of powers and there will be nothing to stop the onrush of this great Oriental invasion.

At the pouring out of the last vial the greatest and mightiest earthquake of all time, accompanied by thunder and lightning, will occur. The great Roman city which is called Babylon will be divided into three parts, all the cities of the world will fall, every island will be destroyed, and great hail will fall from heaven, every stone weighing one hundred pounds, yet men will continue to curse God because of this plague of hail.

This is the fulfillment of all the saucerians' predictions but please note the context—they have no power to escape, these sons of God, devils, demons, and fallen angels. Even their leaders, the dragon, the Roman antichrist, and the false prophet are all recipients of these great cataclysms as God demonstrates His power for all to see. In the final battle of Armageddon, as the whole earth has been changed, Christ returns with His forces and destroys the Satanic power and the evil armies of the earth. Every power and every person join in this final attempt to save themselves by attacking the Lord Jesus Christ. The nineteenth chapter of the book of Revelation describes the power of Jesus Christ, the Creator Himself, as He leads this final event of the tribulation period. He is described in Revelation 19:11-16:

> And I saw heaven opened, and behold a white horse; and he that sat upon him was called Faithful and True, and in righteousness he doth judge and make war.
>
> His eyes were as a flame of fire, and on his head were many crowns; and he had a name written, that no man knew, but he himself.
>
> And he was clothed with a vesture dipped in blood: and his name is called The Word of God.
>
> And the armies which were in heaven followed him upon white horses, clothed in fine linen, white and clean.
>
> And out of his mouth goeth a sharp sword, that with it he should smite the nations: and he shall rule them with a rod of iron: and he treadeth the winepress of the fierceness and wrath of Almighty God.
>
> And he hath on his vesture and on his thigh a name written, King of Kings, and Lord of Lords.

Obviously He comes with all of His power to purge the earth of evil but now it is too late for men to repent. Those who have rejected Him will be condemned to hell, even the powerful false prophet who performed miracles with his Satanic power and the Roman antichrist, the beast, will be judged. Verses 17-21 of Revelation 19 tells us they are to be cast into the lake of fire. Immediately after this great event Christ turns His attention to those people still alive on the earth who have rejected Him. This is the judgment He predicted in Matthew 25:31-46. Those who believe in Him will be spared but those who reject Him will receive Satan's fate. After coming into power Christ will establish His kingdom on this earth. This period ends with the great and mighty battle of Armageddon.

After this period Satan and his followers are bound in chains for a period of one thousand years. At the end of this period of time, known as the "millennium," Satan will be loosed for a season. There will be a final revolt which culminates in the ultimate defeat of Satan and his followers. This final judgment of God terminates their activities forever. Realizing this fact the followers of Satan are massing all of their forces in a great deception in a final attempt to lead as many as possible away from the true God. These fallen angels are therefore appearing unto man in the guise of visitors from other planets. Falsely they predict fulfillment of certain Biblical prophecies and attempt to create the counterfeit happenings necessary to this deception. This is evident by the statements of Oh-Ho concerning the rapture of believers and followers of the saucerians.

They proclaim the coming of Christ but instead tell of the second antichrist, the religious prophet of Rome, who misleads literally millions of people from a belief in Jesus Christ during the tribulation. Without this type of deception people would surely accept the literal truth of the Bible as the events begin to take place around them. Therefore it is necessary for Satan and his followers to proceed on this basis in order to carry out their purpose. Instead of coming in the name of Satan these fallen sons of God claim to be messengers of light or rulers from galactic federations, intelligent beings inhabiting the saucers. They propose to us concepts of great technology in order to help their cause, to lead us down the golden path of acceptance. Claiming to have visited us in the past they take credit for many of the technological advances of humankind. And, in an attempt to confuse us, they appear in many forms, some humanoid, some animal-like, and some spirit. We are told that they have devices that scramble the molecular structure of the brain so they may travel as free spirits. This is an attempt to explain the demonic power of possession that is already attributed to fallen angels. They speak through the mind and it has been said, even by those who fail to believe the Bible or have any concept of the supernatural, that these saucerians possess contactees. Is it any wonder that those who remember such contact under hypnosis speak with robot-like response as if being controlled? The similarities to actual cases of demon possession leave little to the imagination. If this is possession in a new and modern sense and if contactees are being manipulated to present a message that will ultimately deceive mankind, then if we accept the message that man is being visited by beings from outer space and neglect to ask where these beings came from and how they developed their technology we have truly been deceived.

UFOlogists tell us of the return of Jesus Christ in a saucer as they prepare us for a new age of technology. But Jesus Christ does not need a flying saucer because clearly the Bible states that Jesus Christ is the all-mighty, all-powerful Creator of the heavens and the earth. Colossians 1:16–17 tells us "For by him were all things created, that are in heaven, and that are in earth, visible and invisible, whether they be thrones, or dominions, or principalities, or powers: all things were created by him, and for him: And he is before all things, and by him all things consist." In reality nothing came into existence apart from the power and design of Jesus Christ. To accept the saucerians' claim that Jesus Christ is one of them and to support this claim with the Bible totally ignores the true Biblical statements concerning Jesus Christ. No other book claims to hold the key to the ultimate origin of matter. No other book proclaims with certainty that the heavens and the earth were formed by the Word of God. No other book spe-

cifically details the creation of life, man, and time. All
of these things were created by the power of the Creator, Jesus Christ. Ultimately all things will be judged
by this same powerful Creator of the heavens and the
earth. To state that Jesus Christ will return to this earth
in a flying saucer is a total misrepresentation of the
Bible. The one who created the heavens and the earth,
who created the atmosphere and the very air itself, certainly does not need a mechanical vehicle to travel
through space. The one who created, controls, and
holds the atom together certainly has the power to ex-
ercise His dominion over it at will.

Since the Bible specifically states that Jesus Christ is
the power that created all things and is the power that
holds all things together, is it logical to expect Him to
return in a flying saucer? Surely we would expect one
who has the great power to use supernatural means to
accomplish His purpose. As Jesus Christ created all
things and established all the physical laws He also has
the power to change these laws at will. Laying aside
His heavenly attributes He became a man, living a perfect, sinless life with the specific purpose of dying on
the cross for man's sins. His death paid the price of
death for all who would believe in His power. His resurrection from the dead proves His power over death.
He then returned to heaven to sit at the right hand of
God the Father. He warned the world that He would
come again as Judge but promised believers that He
would take them to His heavenly home before the time
of great tribulation. He will come again at the great
battle of Armageddon with power to defeat all the evil
followers of Satan who have been misled and deceived
into following false Christs. Ultimately every person
will be judged in what the Bible says is the Great White
Throne judgment. Those who have believed the truth
will be given eternal life in heaven; those who have rejected the death and resurrection of Jesus Christ will be

cast out. Having chosen to follow evil and to disbelieve God they will be punished with Satan forever.

In the light of the firm Biblical predictions of who Christ is, is it logical to follow Satan instead of Christ? Even now, as the sons of God are upon us preparing for a great invasion and laying the groundwork for a final struggle at Armageddon, whom should we believe and follow? Knowing the outcome of this great battle and realizing the ultimate defeat of Satan that is so vividly predicted in the Holy Scriptures man really has only one choice that would benefit him. Revelation 20:10 states, "And the devil that deceived them was cast into the lake of fire and brimstone, where the beast and the false prophet are, and shall be tormented day and night for ever and ever." Considering the warning and the ultimate punishment and the fact that those who refuse to believe are also judged and cast into the lake of fire with Satan, surely mankind should return to the true Christ and believe.

The weight of the Biblical evidence against the deadly premise that Christ is a saucerian and was manipulated by extraterrestrial visitors is overwhelming. Colossians 1:16—17 states that by Jesus Christ

> were all things created, that are in heaven and that are in earth, visible and invisible [thus covering everything we can physically see], whether they be thrones, or dominions, or principalities, or powers [angels, kingdoms, kings]: all things were created by him, and for him: And he is before all things [Jesus Christ existed before that first chapter of Genesis, before time, matter, or space], and by him all things consist.

Thus we realize the fatal error in following the saucerians, those fallen sons of God.

Paul says of Jesus Christ in Colossians 2:3, "On whom are hid all the treasures of wisdom and knowledge." The root meaning of the word "philosophy" is wisdom; the root meaning in Latin of the word "science" is knowledge. Paul meant that in Jesus Christ are hid all of the treasures of science and philosophy. In other words, you cannot understand anything about the world in which you live apart from understanding and accepting Jesus Christ. You cannot comprehend philosophy apart from Jesus Christ. You cannot discern the true nature of science apart from Jesus Christ. He is the one who created these things, and by Him these things consist.

In our study of the atom we used to think it was composed simply of electrons, protons, and neutrons. We wondered how positively charged protons could exist in the same atomic nucleus and still hold together. We wondered about the fact that the atom was mostly empty space. Now we find that there are many more components than just those three in the atom. Indeed, four forces exist within that atom. There are both attractive and repulsive forces in the nucleus of the atom and no one truly understands the atom or how it is held together. We know that each atom is a complex miniature universe. Man has only begun to comprehend the universe of the small, the level upon which he lives, and the vast universe whose limits are yet far beyond our knowledge. But the Bible tells us that by Jesus Christ all these things consist; He is the power holding the atom together.

But one day Jesus Christ will no longer be occupied in displaying His sustaining power and His love to mankind, but will then stand as Judge. 2 Peter 3:10–14 tells us that when that day comes

the heavens shall pass away with a great noise, and the elements shall melt with fervent heat [an atomic destruction, if you wish, because Jesus Christ can say one word and release the power He possesses over the atom], the earth also and the works that are therein shall be burned up. Seeing then that all these things shall be dissolved, what manner of person ought ye to be in all holy conversation and godliness, Looking for and hasting unto the coming of the day of God, wherein the heavens being on fire shall be dissolved, and the elements shall melt with fervent heat? Nevertheless we, according to his promise, look for new heavens and a new earth, wherein dwelleth righteousness. Wherefore, beloved, seeing that ye look for such things, be diligent that ye may be found of him in peace, without spot, and blameless.

Believers in Jesus Christ need to heed this admonition and realize the power of our blessed Creator and Saviour, Jesus Christ. Those who reject His message will perish just as the sons of God rejected it in time past; they have assuredly chosen the way of destruction.

Is it so strange that there is no empirical evidence that the saucers exist and that the contactees carry with them a missionary fervor to proclaim a new religion? Why is it that they evidence all the signs of possession? Surely we can see these accumulating indications of Satanic power that is taking advantage of man's fear of that which cannot be explained to perpetrate a cosmic fraud on humankind. Even the flying serpent found on the chest emblem of the saucerians has always been attributed to Satan. When we remember that many of the claims of the sighting of saucer people have to be recalled by hypnosis and that the response is robot-like we again see strong evidence of demonism.

This, then, is the key to the mystery of the sons of God—man is being manipulated by outside forces. This manipulation is not by beings from outer planets but by extraterrestrial beings with the ability to fly through the heavens, not with machines but with spiritual power. These demons are deceiving humankind right now; man believes the supertechnological power of these beings who claim to be from outer space. He is listening to their message and ultimately he will pay the price for rejecting the truth. For coming in the guise of angels who claim to prepare the way for the coming of Christ, these sons of God condemn themselves, for the Bible specifically warns of the dangers of heeding any other message than its own revelation. The apostle Paul tells us in Galatians 1:8, "But though we, or an angel from heaven, preach any other gospel unto you than that which we have preached unto you, let him be accursed." So you see, man is not to heed the warning of angels but to heed the revelation of Jesus Christ. There is no need of any other message because all revelation was given in the Word of God. The book of Revelation, which we are told to read and study, admonishes us with these words of warning in Chapter 22, verses 18–20.

For I testify unto every man that heareth the words of the prophecy of this book, If any man shall add unto these things, God shall add unto him the plagues that are written in this book:

And if any man shall take away from the words of the book of this prophecy, God shall take away his part out of the book of life, and out of the holy city, and from the things which are written in this book.

He which testifieth these things saith, Surely I come quickly.

Amen. Even so, come, Lord Jesus.

In this simple warning we are instructed not to heed or believe a message proclaimed by an angel but to believe only the message of the Lord Jesus Christ. The fact that the messengers of Satan, these sons of God, talk of evolutionary beginnings only indicates again the

falsehood of their claims. For the only true message
ever proclaimed by an angel during these end times is
found in Revelation 14:6–7 where the apostle John
records:

> And I saw another angel fly in the midst of heaven,
> having the everlasting gospel to preach unto them that
> dwell on the earth, and to every nation, and kindred,
> and tongue, and people,

> Saying with a loud voice, Fear God, and give glory to
> him; for the hour of his judgment is come: and wor-
> ship him that made heaven, and earth, and the sea,
> and the fountains of waters.

This is the only true message that one can expect from
angelic beings—a message that points to the power of
God the Creator, a message that points to the truth of
Christ. For as Christ created man in the beginning, he
has the power to judge man. When the time is right the
Lord Jesus Christ relinquishing his hold upon the very
atom itself, will destroy the heavens and the earth. All
people will be judged for their belief. People have the
choice of following the true Christ and receiving everlasting life in the glorious beauty of heaven or of following Satan and being condemned. This is the choice
that we have as the sons of God return and promote
the great flying saucer myth.

BIBLIOGRAPHY

Adamski, George. *Flying Saucers Farewell*. London: Abelard-Schuman, 1961.

_____. *Inside the Flying Saucers* (original title: *Inside the Space Ships*). New York: Warner Books, 1967.

Angelucci, Orfeo. *Concrete Evidence*. New York: Flying Saucer News Co., 1959.

Bewitched by the Occult? Denver: B/P Publications (Accent Micro-Books Division), 1973.

Barker, Gray. *Gray Barker's Book of Adamski*. Clarksburg, W.V.: Saucerian Publications, 1970.

Beckley, Timothy Green. *Book of Space Brothers*. Clarksburg, W.V.: Saucerian Publications, 1969.

Berlitz, Charles. *Mysteries from Forgotten Worlds*. New York: Dell, 1972.

Blatty, William Peter. *The Exorcist*. New York: Bantam Books, 1971.

Blum, Ralph with Blum, Judy. *Beyond Earth: Man's Contact With UFOs*. New York: Bantam Books, 1974.

Blumrich, Josef F. *The Spaceship of Ezekiel*. New York: Bantam Books, 1974.

Charroux, Robert. *Forgotten Worlds*. New York: Popular Library, 1971.

Constance, Arthur. *The Inexplicable Sky*. New York: Citadel Press, 1956.

Conway, David. *Magic, an Occult Primer*. New York: Bantam Books, 1972.

DeCamp, L. Sprague. *The Ancient Engineers*. New York: Ballantine Books, 1960.

DeHaan, Richard W. *Satan, Satanism and Witchcraft*. Grand Rapids, Mich.: Zondervan, 1972.

Dione, R. L. *God Drives a Flying Saucer*. New York: Bantam Books, 1969.

Drake, W. Raymond. *Gods and Spacemen in the Ancient East*. New York: Signet Books, New American Library, 1973.

Edwards, Frank. *Stranger Than Science*. New York: Bantam Books, 1959.

_____. *Strange World*. New York: Bantam Books, 1964.

Fuller, John G. *Aliens in the Skies*. New York: G. P. Putnam's Sons, 1966.

_____. *Incident at Exeter: The Story of Unidentified Flying Objects Over America Today*. New York: G. P. Putnam's Sons, 1966.

Girvan, Waveney. *Flying Saucers and Common Sense*. New York: Citadel Press, 1955.

Gurney, Gene and Clare. *Unidentified Flying Objects*. New York: Abelard-Schuman, 1970.

Hall, Donald E. *Satan Enterprises, Inc.* Denver: B/P Publications (Accent Micro-Books Division), 1973.

Keel, John A. *Our Haunted Planet*. Greenwich, Conn.: Fawcett, 1971.

_____. *UFOs Operation Trojan Horse*. New York: G. P. Putnam's Sons, 1970.

Koch, Kurt. *The Devil's Alphabet*. Grand Rapids, Mich.: Fregel Publications, 1969.

Kolosimo, Peter. *Not of This World*. New York: Bantam Books, 1971.

Landsburg, Alan and Sally. *In Search of Ancient Mysteries*. New York: Bantam Books, 1974.

LaVey, Anton Szandor. *The Satanic Bible*. New York: Avon, 1969.

Leslie, Desmond and Adamski, George. *Flying Saucers Have Landed*. New York: British Book Center, 1953.

Lindsey, Hal. *Late Great Planet Earth*. Grand Rapids, Mich.: Zondervan, 1970.

_____. *Satan Is Alive and Well on Planet Earth*. Grand Rapids, Mich.: Zondervan, 1971.

_____. *There's a New World Coming*. Santa Ana, Ca.: Vision House, 1973.

Lovett, C. S. *Dealing With the Devil*. Baldwin Park, Ca.: Personal Christianity, 1967.

Menger, Howard. *From Outer Space* (original title: *From Outer Space to You*). New York: Pyramid Books, 1959.

Michel, Aime. *The Truth About Flying Saucers*. New York: Pyramid Books, 1956.

Demon Experiences in Many Lands. Chicago: Moody Press, 1960.

Norman, Eric. *Gods, Demons and Space Chariots*. New York: Lancer Books, 1972.

_____. *Gods and Devils from Outer Space*. New York: Lancer Books, 1973.

Read, Anne. *Edgar Cayce on Jesus and His Church*. New York: Paperback Library, 1970.

Schafer, J. Bernard. *Flying Saucers*. New York: Flying Saucer News Co., 1970.

Science and Mechanics. Editors, *The Official Guide to UFOs*. New York: Ace, 1968.

Sendy, Jean. *The Coming of the Gods*. New York: Berkley, 1970.

Spencer, John Wallace. *Limbo of the Lost*. New York: Bantam Books, 1969.

Stevic, Milinko S. *Exploration of the Cosmic Space, Parts 1 & 2*, 3rd. ed. New York: Milinko S. Stevic, 1968.

Tomas, Andrew. *We Are Not the First*. New York: Bantam Books, 1971.

Twitchell, Paul. *Eckankar the Key to Secret Worlds*. San Diego, Ca.: Illuminated Way Press, 1969.

Von Daniken, Erich. *Chariots of the Gods* New York: Bantam Books, 1968.

_____. *Gods from Outer Space*. New York: Bantam Books, 1968.

Whitney, David C., ed. *Flying Saucers*. New York: Cowles Communications, 1967.

Wilburn, Gary A. *The Fortune Sellers*. Glendale, Ca.: G/L Publications, 1972.

Wilkins, H. T. *Flying Saucers Uncensored*. New York: Pyramid Publications, 1955.

Willis, Charles D. *End of Days: 1971–2001*. Jericho, N. Y.: Exposition Press, 1972.

Wilson, Clifford. *Crash Go the Chariots*. New York: Lancer Books, 1972.

Young, Mort. *UFO Top Secret*. New York: Essandess Special Editions, Simon and Schuster, 1967.

READ ALL ABOUT IT !!!

The Great Tribulation...the Rapture... the Mark of the Beast... the Antichrist...the Second Coming.

The most puzzling and least understood book of the Bible—Revelation—is explained and clarified in these prophetic and eye-opening books:

- __IN THE TWINKLING OF AN EYE. One of the most startling novels in the annals of Christian literature. *Watson.* 75¢ paper

- __THE MARK OF THE BEAST. A fictional account of the reign of the Antichrist. *Watson.* 95¢ paper

- __RAPTURED. The terrifying story of those left behind to suffer in the time of Tribulation. *Angley.* $1.25 paper

- __THE VISION. A famous author unfolds a vision of the future that is starting to happen today! *Wilkerson.* $1.50 paper

- __HOW TO SURVIVE THE COMING CALAMITY. A message of hope—not despair—for all Christians. *Wilkerson.* $1.50 paper

---

ORDER FROM YOUR BOOKSTORE

If your bookstore does not stock these books, order from
SPIRE BOOKS
Box 150, Old Tappan, New Jersey 07675

Please send me the books I've checked above. Enclosed is my payment plus 25¢ mailing charge on first book ordered, 10¢ each additional book.

NAME_____

STREET_____

CITY_____ STATE_____ ZIP_____
__Amount enclosed. __Cash. __Check. __Money order. (No c.o.d.'s)

S-13